MW01602325

Mountain Whispers

A humble story of friendship, perseverance, and inspiration found hiking in the White Mountains

C. David Bousquet & Scott Tetreault

ISBN-9798361676743

Dedication

This book is dedicated to our families, particularly our parents for always inspiring us to be the best we could be.

Thanks to all the folks who offered input and support as we put this memory together and our friends and family who accompanied us on many of these adventures.

Special thanks to Rodney Blais for providing the majority of the photographs in this book, and to Jessica LaMountain for being a thoughtful and thorough reader and editor as we put this together.

Table of Contents

Preface

The White Mountains of New Hampshire encompass the majority of the northern portion of the state and a small part of eastern Maine. They are part of the northern Appalachian Mountains and are easily the most rugged mountains in New England. Most of the area is public land, specifically the White Mountain National Forest as well as numerous New Hampshire State Parks. Within the Whites are multiple mountain ranges, notably the Presidential Range, the Franconia Range, the Sandwich Range, the Carter-Moriah Range, and the Kinsman Range. In all, there are 48 peaks in New Hampshire that exceed an elevation of 4000 feet and are collectively known as the "Four Thousand Footers".

Because of their rugged beauty and proximity to the population centers of New England and southern Canada, the Whites are heavily visited year-round by tourists, campers, skiers, hikers and even bikers during the annual motorcycle week every summer in Laconia. It is the hikers and adventurers who get off the beaten tracks, away from the crowds and amusements and noise and instead venture into the woods to challenge themselves; those who feel the draw of the wilderness and the quiet and peace it offers.

Within this group is a much smaller group who look up at a peak and wonder what it would be like up there, to look down into the valleys and the world below. With 48 peaks scattered throughout the region the options are many and varied and on any given day one could find themselves hard pressed to even find a parking spot at some of the most popular trailheads. Yet for one willing to travel a bit deeper and farther on the back roads, there are many trails that will offer solitude and quiet. It is likely impossible to know how many people summit any given peak in any one year, nor how many have done multiple peaks over the years but suffice to say it is many tens of thousands.

The Appalachian Trail runs across the spine of these mountains as it wends its' way north to Mount Katahdin in Maine and south to Springer Mountain in Georgia. Typically, in spring you will come across thru hikers heading south, traversing the remaining snowfields in the higher elevations as they are making their way towards warmer weather. Then in the fall, as the colors are fading from the slopes you will find hikers hurrying their way north to try to beat the onset of winter as they finish their 2,195-mile end to end trek. It is an amazing feat of endurance and perseverance and a life's list accomplishment. Invariably, if asked, many of the northbound hikers after having walked the length of the Appalachian chain to this point will tell you the roughest and most rugged part of their walk was in the White Mountains. That is a major testament to the ruggedness of this region.

There is another sub-group of people who summit these peaks. The people who climb one, maybe two…. then feel compelled to try another…then another. They read more about this peak or that peak and have to try it again. Eventually they have five or six peaks under their belt and the hook is set. The idea begins to percolate. "Why not do them all?" And a personal quest takes root; a thirst is generated that cannot be satisfied until they are all done.

These are the Four Thousand Footers. The Peakbaggers. The people who would forego a trip to the Caribbean to instead climb a peak or two or three over a few days in pouring rain and get eaten alive by bugs and slog thru mud to set up a tent and eat freeze dried beef stroganoff and be more than happy about it.

As of the beginning of 2020, over 15,000 people (and 380 dogs) had completed all 48 peaks according to the 4000 Footer Club of the Appalachian Mountain Club. This seemingly large number should in no manner trivialize the accomplishment. The time, effort and drive to summit and descend each peak on foot in this unforgiving terrain is by no means a small feat. The people who accept the challenge come from all walks of life. Young or old(er), professional or clerk or blue collar, mothers and daughters. People who have done little hiking in their lives up to this point or others who have walked the Pacific Crest Trail or the Appalachian Trail (or both!). There are people who get them all in one year or people like me and my companion who take several years.

Then you find the "extremists". The very small group of hardy souls that decide to hike each peak in each month of the year. For example, they will summit Mount Lafayette in March. Then perhaps in September. Then again in January until it has been summited twelve times. 48 peaks twelve times each…...576 successful summits!!! This feat is called the Grid…. And the people who manage to pull it off are affectionately called "Gridiots" for not-so-subtle reasons. This group counts a total of roughly eighty people and their fiefdom is the "Gridiocracy".

And you have the Direttissima. The goal is to summit all 48 peaks on foot in one continuous hike without any outside assistance. No shuttles. No food resupplies. On you own. The trip spans roughly 240 miles and over 80,000 feet of elevation gain depending on route selection and obviously is only for the most durable and best conditioned hikers. The number of finishers is estimated to be around ten people. Ten amazing people.

The variety of challenges is nearly limitless.

This book will be an account of the travels, the experiences and circumstances and the lessons learned that two close friends discovered while climbing the 48 peaks. It will hopefully provide an insight into what may cause one to decide to initiate such an undertaking as well as an account of the growth, physically and spiritually that one can expect. It is a story of camaraderie and support and the formation of lifelong friendships.

Come for a walk in the woods. We hope you enjoy the journey and the company. *Dave*

Introduction

"The world is big, and I want to have a good look at it before it gets dark"
John Muir

Scott:

How did we get here? Not totally sure, but Dave and I made a pact as we were traversing the iconic Franconia Ridge peering toward Mt Lafayette that we would hike all 48 four thousand footers in the White Mountains. This was our 5th mountain to date, and we were once again in awe of the beauty of these mountains, in particular this magnificent ridge walk. We were not sure if we had the physical ability, equipment, or ample knowledge of the area, and possibly underestimated all three. However, we were resolute in our decision and committed to this endeavor regardless of how long it may take.

I'm not sure why we made this huge commitment. It started with a love of nature, the outdoors, and the love of the White Mountains in New Hampshire. Possibly I was looking for a new venture, a new hobby and something to share with my son, who had shown a real interest in climbing mountains. Or it was just the thing a couple of life-long friends could do in their spare time. Most likely a combination of all these factors, but in any case, it was a sound plan, one we both felt strongly about.

Initially, I'm not sure either one of us were ready for such a venture. Personally, I struggled with my physical stamina and mental focus on the first few climbs. Dave was out of shape and going through a rough time personally. Underestimation for sure. We soon discovered that we lacked proper equipment, lacked navigation skills, and needed to prepare better for each individual trip, including keeping a much closer eye on mountain weather conditions. That never discouraged us, and with our resolve intact, we continued to make necessary improvements and gradually became more confident, capable hikers in a rather short matter of time.

We soon found ourselves doing up to seven or eight peaks a year, whatever our schedules allowed. We camped overnight in tent shelters, pushed ourselves on more strenuous climbs, with better preparation and much better equipment. Confidence replaced uncertainty, and this confidence fueled our determination and drive to "bag" all of them. At no point did we ever think of quitting. We had been poured on, snowed on, fallen into rivers, waded through mud bogs and gotten lost; I had been at my absolute point of exhaustion on numerous occasions. I had lost my wallet and locked my keys in the car. We had a bear encounter, yet despite these trials and tribulations at no time did Dave of I ever think of quitting.

What you will read about in this book are the experiences of a couple of friends spending time together in the mountains. The lessons we learned through the years are life-long; the things we learned about ourselves carried over into our personal lives. The positive experiences left me wanting more; the agony of a steep, rugged climb to a beautiful summit and a seeming non-ending descent were soon forgotten. We would begin to plan our next trip immediately after; relentless in our study of the White Mountain Guide, Dave and I would have numerous discussions as to trail selection, date and time, and camping preparation. It became clockwork. To this day, I still study trails, prepare hikes with the enthusiasm of a younger hiker. I no longer tackle strenuous hikes, choosing to focus on smaller, more accessible peaks throughout New Hampshire. (52 With a View).

Dave and I have summitted all 48 mountains over 4000 ft in the White Mountains. We have walked over 300 miles on almost 90 different trails averaging 10.6 miles per hike and achieved elevation gains of over 100,000 feet throughout Northern New Hampshire. We have stayed at six different AMC huts, and 2 Randolph Mountain Club huts. We have frequented 9 different campgrounds and had two bear encounters, one moose meeting and drank more beers than could be counted. These hikes have taken us 30 plus trips from Connecticut to New Hampshire; I have hiked with my father, my wife, my daughter, my son, my brother, my uncle, nephews, and too many friends to mention.

I cannot put into words how these experiences added to my life. Hiking is an individual sport; the battle is from within. But the reward is worth it; whether it was the absolute silence on the top of a mountain in peak foliage season, or the beauty of a mountain stream or waterfall, the memories linger on forever. Each hike was uniquely difficult in a number of ways. The sense of accomplishment in the completion of each and every hike would be celebrated after each climb. Plop down in a chair, take the boots off, and sip a few cold beverages. What a feeling. Maybe that is why we did it after all.

Dave:

What drew me back to the White Mountains? With the exception of a few little family trips when my children were younger, I hadn't really spent much time in the area for several years. I was certainly familiar with the beauty of the White Mountain National Forest and the attractions, having spent quite a considerable amount of time camping and exploring in my younger days of college adventures. However, I had never considered climbing any of the peaks with the notable exception of Mount Washington, which as the tallest and most famous holds all the allure.

That is not to say that I hadn't done my share of hiking. I had been fortunate enough when younger to have travelled a bit and had the opportunity to explore and hike in such places as Rocky Mountain National Park, Mesa Verde, the Grand Canyon, and Yosemite and to marvel at the natural scenic beauty across the country. However, as one gets older and more "responsible", family and career come along, and often such pursuits are set aside.

In the summer of 1999, my life was changing significantly as I was going through a divorce and I found myself adrift, not really knowing what the future would throw at me as I tried to rebuild my life. I had spent a fair amount of time with my oldest and closest friend Scott, doing some local hiking and fishing and enjoying the time being outdoors more. It was around this time that Scott brought up the subject of a trip to New Hampshire "like the old days", but this time maybe consider climbing a mountain while we were there. Sounded as good an idea as any to me so we set about falling into something we never expected, a quest. An adventure that would take years. A commitment that would change us forever.

It started slowly, and sometimes painfully as the idea began to coalesce into something tangible, but once the hook was set, there was no escaping or denying the feeling that this HAD to be done. It was like an itch you can't stop scratching sometimes because it hurts so good.

One successful summit of a peak became two, then three and early on the die was cast: on a windswept day on Franconia Ridge, Scott and I decided we were going to climb all the 48 peaks over 4000 feet in the White Mountains.

It became evident early on that there was a LOT to learn. From the obvious, like map reading and navigation, proper gear, food and hydration and proper preparation for each venture, to the less evident, intangible things like mental toughness, physical prowess, and a good old stick to it attitude. All of these did not happen at once, and often a lesson may have been taught by a mountain that was perhaps forgotten or overlooked and it was then reinforced by another peak. Over time however, peak after peak we got better and better at it and despite some mishaps along the way Scott and I became solid Peakbaggers as a couple of middle-aged guys.

As the trips continued, we were able to bring others into the circle and help introduce them to what we were doing. It was always great to have another person or more along to enjoy the beauty and challenge of what we had started. In all, over the years we summitted peaks with at least eighteen other people, a couple of whom (Rodney and Don) went on to complete their own list of the 48 peaks and we helped inspire others who are now in their own pursuit.

None of this happened quickly. Scott and I summitted our first peak in the summer of '99 and didn't stand atop our 48th until 2012. But over that time, I'd like to think we became better people. Better stewards of the wilderness. More open to change and opportunity. Better friends to the people around us. Stronger. Personally, the mountains helped me heal from the hurt and anger that had grown in me for many years prior. I relearned the rejuvenating power of nature and being in the forest or standing atop a mountain.

Throughout this book, we will try to impart some of the lessons we were taught by the trails and the peaks. Not all will learn the same lessons or a similar takeaway, but I have come to believe that each adventure one undertakes will offer something in the way of a revelation, either about themselves, or the world around us. I hope that it may encourage others to try to step outside their comfort zone and in so doing also change them in some   positive   way.   It's   worth   it.

1. Mount Madison

"The Mountains are Calling, and I Must Go"
John Muir

Early Summer 1999

"Caution: The section of this trail on the headwall of Madison Gulf is one of the most difficult in the White Mountains, going over several ledge outcrops, bouldery areas and a chimney with loose rock.... allow extra time, and do not start up the headwall late in the day. The ascent time of the headwall may require several hours more than the allotted time...." (White Mountain Guide 28th Edition)

Scott had called Dave and casually mentioned that he was hoping for a trip to the White Mountains and was curious if Dave needed a break from the routine and wanted to go along to climb a peak. At the time Dave really had nothing particular going on so he figured a change of scenery would be great and recalling the many camping trips in the mountains the two had done many years before, he jumped at the chance to get away and spend some time outdoors.

To this day, they weren't really sure why they chose to hike Mount Madison. This would be their first effort to climb any mountain other than Washington, which they had done over the years; Scott with his son Mike, and Dave with a college class in the '70's. Madison seemed as good as any other peak to do for as with many hikers the bigger and higher peaks hold all the allure. Scott had been doing some research and was curious to try utilizing the Appalachian Mountain Club backcounty hut system, which offered food and shelter to hikers at higher elevations. Mike had shown solid hiking ability when he and his father did Washington, showing the stamina and determination of youth. He and his best friend Eric eagerly jumped on board for this trip. The two older guys did pay some rudimentary attention to the things they were "supposed" to bring along on such a hike, but the habit of overpacking was hard to break and they carried too much weight and unnecessary nonsense for a hike of this nature. They had a map and had given a cursory glance at the Guide, but, in reality, they didn't know what they were in for.

They made their reservations for the Madison Hut and overstuffed their metal frame packs with sleeping bags, extra clothing, too much food (although Scott did make an excellent trail mix), a few bottles of water, a basic map purchased from the Mountain Wanderer shop in Lincoln, and first aid kit as they set off on the Great Gulf Trail in blissful ignorance on their way to the summit of Mt. Madison.

The hike started off with relative ease, meandering through the hardwoods without any significant elevation gain. When they reached an intersection on the Great Gulf Trail, they paused a moment to look at the map to determine the "best" way to reach the hut. They opted to take the Madison Gulf Trail because it seemed to be the shortest route to the summit. Real map reading skills would have been invaluable in making this decision, but they continued the hike not really knowing what to expect up ahead.

Bridge to Great Gulf Wilderness

Now, Scott had played in a golf tournament the day before they set out, consuming a fair amount of alcohol, eating fried crap, and doing a poor job of hydration, which is not a good foundation to build a hike upon. As they moved deeper into the Great Gulf Wilderness the trail steepened greatly and without relent. Scott began to get very winded and had to stop frequently to catch his breath. The fact was that he was not in good hiking condition and after the festivities of the day before dehydration was creeping in. Those two factors, coupled with some anxiety of not knowing anything about the trail ahead or the time it would take formed a near perfect storm of worry, affecting both his physical and mental stamina. He was hitting the wall both figuratively and literally. It got to a point where he was so engrossed in his own state that he didn't care to maintain any sense of how the others in the group were handling the hike. It seemed that every step, every steep pitch was daunting. He tried rest, drinking, and eating a few handfuls of trail mix despite having no appetite, and he plodded on. Dave could see that Scott was having difficulty. Mike and Eric had bounced off ahead as one would expect two young friends in the mountains would do, but Dave cautioned them to stay within shouting distance while he assisted Scott. The headwall of the glacial cirque loomed ahead through the trees, and it wasn't going to be easy for any of them. There were some sections of the trail where Dave relieved Scott of his heavy pack to lighten his load as he climbed. The boys wisely waited at one particularly rough scramble over some ledges for Scott and Dave to catch up while Scott dug deeply for whatever grit and determination he had left. To him, the others seemed to be doing much better and he used their example to help pull him to the top of the headwall. Dave scouted out a decent route and went ahead first to make sure the boys could handle it and then waited on top for each one to surmount the obstacle. Then, he went back down to grab Scotts pack and scrambled about halfway up to a point where he could throw it up to Mike. Back down again to talk Scott through getting up and over the hurdle. It was slow and painful, but he found the strength and made it to the top. Relieved after they accomplished that task, they took a short break and soldiered on.

Scott achieves the top of the headwall!

When they finally achieved the top of the headwall and the intersection with the Parapet Trail, they saw that there was still snow in the shaded areas where drifts had built up over the winter. They could see Star Lake off to the left and despite the cloud in Scotts head he was greatly relieved as he knew the hut was not too far off. Dave had sent the younger men ahead to alert the hut "croo" that there was a hiker in some distress coming up the trail. This proved to be the first experience Dave and Scott would have with a hut "croo" and they were amazing. Mike and Eric had gotten to the hut a few moments before Dave and as he approached there were already several members geared up and heading out to get Scott. They asked Dave where he was and once informed that he was coming up near Star Lake they were off in a flash to find him. They met up with him within minutes and walked him to the hut where they set about getting him rehydrated with electrolytes and had him rest in a bunk for a while to drink and eat a protein bar. After about half an hour his head began to clear and strength was coming back into his legs, feeling much more stable under his weight.

A word about the hut "croos" as they are affectionately called: These are teams of mostly college-aged kids who feed, entertain, teach, and occasionally assist hikers and overnight guests in the AMC's eight backcountry huts. They tend to the cooking, cleaning, hauling in of food and staples and hauling out trash several times a week and have the times of their lives doing it. They come from colleges and universities across the country to spend their summers in this world of beauty and challenge in a totally unique culture and environment and they take their experience very seriously but have a great deal of fun while tending to business. Dave marveled and commented on how fast they mobilized and brought Scott to the hut and tended to him. He regretted that when he was younger, he didn't know much about the AMC's huts and if he had would likely have tried to join a croo.

As Scott recovered, the group knew there was still one issue: they hadn't summited Mt. Madison yet! There was still about a mile to go to accomplish the goal of the day. Scott was a bit embarrassed, and his pride was in tatters, but he was feeling strong enough to complete the task with the hiking party that had supported him thus far. He was determined to finish the job that he had started. *Ask yourself: "Can I give more?" The answer is usually: "Yes."* That afternoon the four set out for the last steep stretch up to the summit.

Mountain Whispers

Being on top of any of the peaks in the Presidential range is an uplifting, almost euphoric experience. After a long day on the trail Scott stood atop the 5,367-foot mountain with his son and his buddy and his hiking partner, his oldest and dearest friend, and the feeling made all the pain and agony worthwhile. They sat up there with a croo member taking a break as the sun began to get low in the sky, chatting about the New England Patriots and just soaking in the breeze and mood of a mountain top on a beautiful day.

They descended back to the hut, threw off the hiking shoes and got into some clean clothes and comfortable footwear and relaxed in the great room, playing cards while chatting with other hikers about the trails they had taken and what their plans for the next day were. Another somewhat unique thing about the huts is that many folks who stay at them are usually a little older. The younger hikers might stop at a hut to refill their water and maybe grab a snack, but most often will go out and camp in the bush somewhere, but the huts are often patronized by folks who are long time AMC members who have had their share of nights in the woods but now prefer the adventures of a climb but with a nice reward at the end in the form of a great meal and a soft bunk. The huts are an excellent way to do exactly that.

The croo put out an excellent and hearty meal for all with the only caveat being, "Take all you want, but eat all you take." Hauling garbage down a 4000+ foot peak on a hot summer day can't be any fun. The gang collapsed into their bunks for a well-deserved rest after the day's work. One would think that after such a day that sleep would be deep and restful, however shortly after midnight that changed as a mountain thunderstorm reared up and put on a light and sound extravaganza unlike anything they had seen before or since. They rose from their respective bunks to go to the wide windows of the great room and watched the lightning dancing off the mountains and the thunder crashing immediately after in a show of natures' amazing power. Someone near muttered about how good it was to be safe and dry.

The next morning the group was awakened early by the smell of coffee wafting through the hut and the sound of a croo member playing guitar and the rest of his mates singing the Grateful Dead song, "Wake Up to Find Out That You Are the Eyes of the World." A breakfast of eggs, muffins, home fries, juice and coffee followed shortly after to fortify the hikers for the day and after packing their gear were out the door by 8:00 AM.

They knew they would not be descending via the Madison Gulf Trail, instead they had chosen to walk the Parapet Trail north to the Osgood Trail and descend the ridge back down into the Great Gulf Wilderness. This is a section of the Appalachian Trail, and they were not disappointed in their choice. As they descended the Osgood from Madison they paused to take in the breathtaking view of Mt. Washington to their south. The summit was socked in by the only clouds in the sky. *It was one of those moments that each hike offers to those who pay attention; a moment turned into a lasting memory and further stokes the flames within to consider hiking more.* There was a warm wind blowing from the east that day to inspire their refreshed legs to make good time as they worked their way towards the Great Gulf Trail and eventually to the car to take them home.

As they walked, Scott and Dave began to compile a mental list of not only what they had accomplished, but also what they had done wrong and how they needed to adjust their preparations and planning should they decide to do this again. *The fact is that mountains teach one modesty.* There are so many factors that contribute to or detract from a successful hike and this being their first they experienced some of each. The good: one's choice of hiking partners is crucial to not only enjoying a hike but also to know that one is with someone they can count on if needed. Setting realistic, but challenging goals to push one out of one's comfort zone and to have to earn the reward. Self-care before, during and after a rough hike and hydration is crucial. Eating properly and fueling up with foods that will sustain one through a journey. These concepts don't necessarily all come at once in some great epiphany, but after a few lessons from the mountains they become second nature.

Before they had even left the trail, Dave and Scott were discussing what they wanted to do next.

2. Southern Presidentials

"I go to nature to be soothed and healed, and to have my senses put in order"
John Burroughs

July 2000

Coming off their trip up Madison in '99, and after much discussion Scott and Dave decided to attempt a traverse of the southern Presidential Range by "following history" and travelling via the Crawford Path, arguably the oldest continually maintained footpath in the United States. This trail was cut through this rugged terrain by Abel Crawford and his son Ethan Allen Crawford in 1819! Scott was thinking to himself as they began heading up the rugged path, "Didn't these guys have anything better to do with their time in the New Hampshire mountains in 1819?"

This walk would require the men to summit three peaks in the Presidential Range: Mount Pierce, Mount Eisenhower, and Mount Monroe over a distance of roughly eight miles with the day ending at the Lake of the Clouds Hut for an overnight stay. They had a very positive experience at the Madison Hut the year before, enjoying the food, the ambiance, and the opportunity to rest their weary legs overnight before the trip down the next day.

Mike and Eric rejoined the crew as they drove up the day before and camped in Crawford Notch, and they began their day relatively early on a hot and humid, but clear July morning. Hoping not to make the "Madison Mistake" of improper fueling and hydration they enjoyed a pasta dinner the night before and kept alcohol consumption to a minimum.

Next morning, they started up the path towards Pierce knowing more of what to expect, having digested the White Mountain Guide and thoroughly studying the map. By their rudimentary calculations and being that they were still learning about the time estimates in the Guide and gauging their own hiking speed, they figured they would be atop Pierce in about two hours.

Dave was thinking to himself that the Crawford's did their job well. There was no denying this was a beautiful trail. They followed Gibbs Brook for the first mile or so on a gentle ascent along the bank. They were feeling good to be back out in the woods again as the road sounds faded away and only the chatter of the boys and their footfalls could be heard. They soon diverged away from Gibbs Brook and the trail steepened considerably and presented uneven rock steps through the hardwoods. Dave wondered aloud to no one in particular if this was perhaps some of the original work of the Crawford's. He wanted to believe it was.

Feeling strong, they passed the cut-off to the Mitzpah Springs Hut and made straight for Mt. Pierce. They were still in the woods and there would be no rest until the first peak was under their belts today. The trail stayed steep, only starting to level off a bit as the trees became thinner near the summit. As they broke through, the vastness of the Presidential Range stretched out before them to the north. Inspiring is not a strong enough description. The blue sky was peppered with fluffy fair-weather clouds that dappled the peaks of Eisenhower, Franklin, and Monroe. Just beyond Monroe loomed Mt. Washington's peak bathed in sunshine. They achieved the 4,293-foot summit of Mt. Pierce almost exactly two hours into the trip and rested a bit and enjoyed a snack.

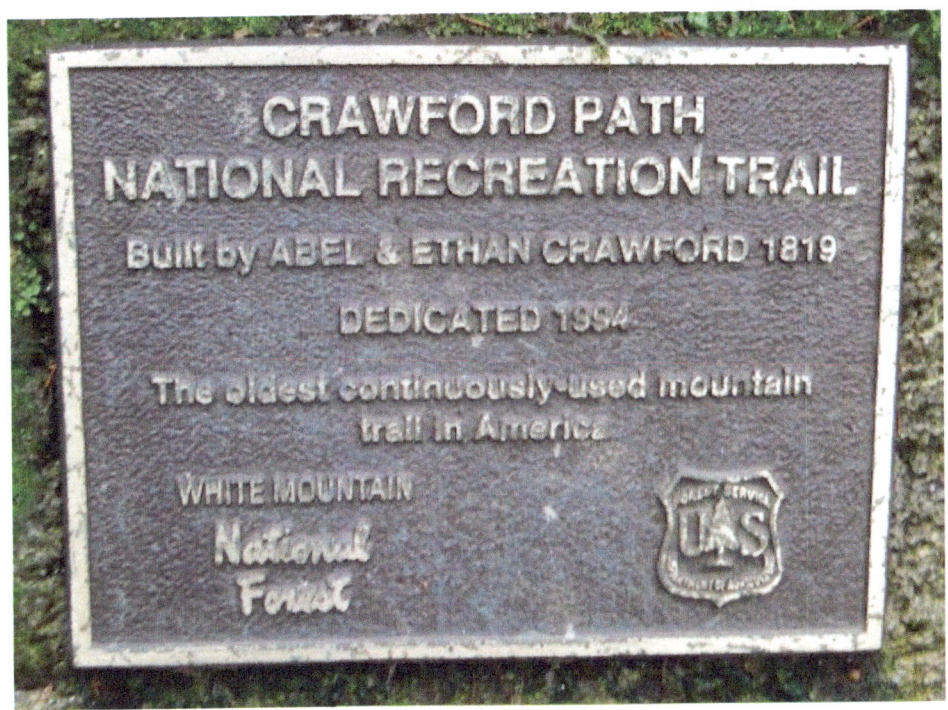

Crawford Path Marker

The summit of Pierce afforded nice views and the crew could see the remaining peaks laid out before them in the breathtaking landscape. They all knew they had much more hard work ahead of them, but they understood it would be worth the effort. However, for Scott the heat and humidity were beginning to have an effect, at first subtly, but as they continued onward it became more pronounced, and he could tell that his stamina was becoming an issue. As they neared the cutoff to the Eisenhower Loop leading to that summit he and Dave stopped and took a break to determine the best way to proceed. They were carrying the Guide with them, making them better equipped to consider all their options. Dave could see Scott was starting to tire and having become a student of the Guide, suggested they skirt Eisenhower and stay on the Crawford Path to eliminate that elevation gain for now and instead grab Eisenhower on the way back tomorrow. In Scotts mind it made great sense to him as his confidence was a bit shaken again, but he also knew that quitting was not an option. This became another one of those good decisions during the course of many trips that enable them to push forward and adapt as needed on the fly. They were learning that so many factors play into a successful hiking adventure: hydration, food intake, and so very importantly, state of mind. As they continued up the trail Scott pulled a banana from his pack and wolfed it down, which offered him a burst of energy and a feeling of renewed strength. Maybe it was the potassium and some extra water and rest that helped give him a second life as they walked. The bottom line is *it's ok to slow down and take a break.* Whatever it was, he forged into the remaining leg of the journey, and they all pressed on and covered the mile or so to Mount Franklin quickly. Franklin is listed at an elevation of 5,004 feet but does not count as a 4000-footer amazingly because it is considered a "shoulder" of nearby Mount Monroe. Detail, details.... more on that later.

The Loop Trail

They blew right over Franklin and about a half-mile later they all stood atop 5,372-foot Mt. Monroe, approximately 7.5 miles into their walk, gazing eastward and down into Oakes Gulf and then turning northward towards Washington. The whistle of the Cog Railway was echoing across the terrain, and they could see several hikers making their way towards Washington's summit on the final stretch of the Crawford Path from the Lakes of the Clouds Hut below. They covered the less than half-mile down to the hut quickly and got themselves checked in and planned to while the rest of the afternoon away.

Mike and Eric however, had other plans. They were each 15 years old and had no intentions of just sitting around the hut for a few hours with a couple of "old men". They were in no way going to allow themselves to be so close to Washington and not go grab the summit. They stayed with Scott and Dave for only about 15 minutes after arrival at the hut before they were off again. The two older men watched the youngsters ascend the slope of Washington on the Crawford Path for about ten minutes before losing sight of them and then turned back to getting themselves comfortable. A change of clothes, some comfortable sneakers, select their bunks for the night and then grab a cup of coffee.

Dave amused himself for about an hour by poring through the collection of guest logbooks on the bookshelves and was actually able to find his name from his last stay at Lakes in 1977! Way back then he was taking a class called "Geography of New England" at Eastern Connecticut State College and part of that class included a trip to New Hampshire and a climb of Washington. He recalled it as being a great class with a good group of people and a great professor as he enjoyed remembering the time from his younger days. Meanwhile, Scott was chatting with a couple of other hikers, who also arrived at the hut early, so Dave put the logbooks away, stepped outside and wandered off to find a comfortable rock to sit on.

As he sat staring into the distance, he began to think about what he was doing. Not just in the immediate and physical sense but in a deeper and more philosophical manner. He was never really one to get too "in touch with his feelings", because he was either too busy tending to whatever life put in front of him, or perhaps simply not interested in "going there". Sure, here he was, essentially sitting on top of a mountain, hiking with his team, and the day had already been a success. Yet he got the notion that he was doing more than just the task at hand in the here and now. There were new thought processes stirring. There was a healing occurring. An education was commencing. And he liked what was

13

happening. *The mountains can open your mind and soul to feelings that were previously not known or felt.*

Eric and Mike returned from the summit of Washington a couple hours later and they all settled into the hut for a great AMC dinner and entertainment by the croo. The hut was at capacity of 90 guests and the entire group was happy and energetic as people played cards, backgammon, or chess as darkness fell. A couple of the more seasoned hikers actually had a spare Nalgene or two filled with their favorite wine or beverage of choice for the evening. Needless to say, Scott and Dave made a mental note of that custom.

As the hut was starting to settle down for the night, a sound like thunder or an explosion echoed up from the valley. People were rushing to the windows or outdoors to look as another retort echoed. Fireworks! Our small band hadn't really given too much thought to the date, but it happened to be 4th of July weekend and what they were hearing were fireworks being launched at the Mount Washington Hotel down in the notch at Bretton Woods! Rushing outside, the four guys found a spot just below the hut and they had the extremely unique opportunity to view pyrotechnics display from above! They were sitting at an elevation of about 5000 feet and the fireworks appeared to be detonating at about 2000 feet and certainly was not something your casual picnicker sees every day. This put a really nice exclamation point on the day as they moved back inside to get some well-earned rest.

Next morning, they were awakened by the croo's early morning serenade and enjoyed breakfast and coffee before packing the gear and heading out to retrace their steps on the Crawford Path. Completely refreshed, they made short work of getting back up to the summit of Monroe then blew right over Franklin and diverged onto the Eisenhower Loop to grab the peak they skirted around the previous day. They passed the junction with Edmunds Path and made the top of Eisenhower at 4,760-feet in a gentle breeze. There were only a few hikers at the summit at this early hour including a couple who had spent the night at the hut also. Discussion about the cool fireworks show ensued when a guy came running northbound up to the summit and was gone before anyone could even say hello. This was a glimpse of one of the crazy people who get their perverse pleasures by running these trails and making the old guys look bad. Who knows if he was doing a full Presi Traverse, a "simple" morning run, or perhaps even a Diretissima attempt? Either way Dave turned to Scott and mentioned he was impressed, but still preferred to take it slow and easy....

The day was young and the four lingered around the huge cairn atop Eisenhower, taking in the views on a clear day before reloading their pack and heading southbound and down.

As they were nearing Pierce, they came upon a group of hikers standing on the trail near a small ledge. Getting nearer, they soon ascertained that this group was assisting another person who apparently had a nasty slip and fall right at that ledge and had injured her leg and ankle pretty badly. She was in definite pain, and it was obvious that she would not be getting down off this mountain unassisted. Scott asked if they could help in any way, and they thanked him but refused. Apparently, another member of the party had already turned around and headed down to alert a rescue team. Keep in mind, these were still the days when universal cell phone coverage was still very rare. *Remember, not everything is within your control.*

The fellows wished them the best of luck and carried on over Pierce and back down into the trees. They hadn't gone a mile when they came to the first of the rescuers heading up the trail with a heavy pack, taking a quick breather. Dave spoke with him briefly and asked how often he must hump up these trails to assist people in distress. His response before soldiering on, "This time of year, at least three or four times a week." *The dedication and selflessness of these people and groups who put their own wellbeing and comfort aside to help people in trouble is admirable and commendable.*

The trail wound down through the rocks and trees as Scott and Dave made their own pace, the boys having blown them away in their own mad scramble out. They soon came upon Gibbs Brook again and shortly after broke out and walked across the road to the Highland Center lot. Feeling good about their efforts the older members were craving a frosty cold brew but in the near ultimate of rookie mistakes had neglected to pack the cooler with ice for their liquid reward! Not to be deterred, they quaffed a couple of lukewarm Bud Lights and reflected on the trek.

Dave and Scott were early along in their mountain adventures in New Hampshire; still inexperienced but honing their skills with each new hike. A 2-day, 16 mile trek, bagging three prominent peaks in the prestigious Presidential Range was a solid effort, and one that set the tone for future endeavors. These mountains, some of the most iconic in New Hampshire, were teaching both, all they had to do was pay attention and learn. Each peak presents its own unique set of difficulties, testing hikers physically and mentally. In the clean, fresh air, each hiker learns to be diligent in both research and preparation, necessities for any successful venture on foot. The most glaring wisdom imparted to the guys by the mountains on this particular trip was that of injury prevention. Witnessing a hiker in obvious pain and in need of assistance from a rescue team is a humbling experience; a lesson both men vowed never to duplicate. Unfortunately, accidents and injuries are sometimes inevitable. Focus, planning, and equipment go a long way to promote individual safety, and this was a loud and clear message they carried with them throughout the remainder of their hikes in the White Mountains. An unforeseen yet clear takeaway from this experience was the eternal respect and admiration for the volunteer crews who assist injured or lost hikers in these mountains. Kudos to these inspirational men and women.

On a much less serious note, the final, less important lesson learned on these 2 days hiking in July was to make sure the liquid refreshments are properly iced before departure. Scott and Dave did not need that reminder   ever   again.

3. Franconia Loop

"If you can't be in awe of Mother Nature, there is something wrong with you"
Alex Trebek

Summer 2002

Our hikers found themselves too wrapped up in the vagaries and daily business of Life to get to the White Mountains in 2001 and they were not happy about it at all. They vowed that another year would not go by without escaping to a place they had loved and enjoyed for so much of their lives. After the successful southern Presidential trip with Mike and Eric two summers before, they began 2002 looking for more adventures. They had learned their lesson from Mt. Madison: *Read the guidebook and pay attention to the map!* However, their desire for "epic" had not abated and they decided to tackle one of the most iconic walks in all the White Mountains, the Franconia Loop.

There are a couple of ways this loop can be tackled; if going counterclockwise one can go up the Liberty Spring Trail or Falling Waters Trail to Franconia Ridge and head north, or if going clockwise the option is the Old Bridle Trail to the Greenleaf Trail up to Mt. Lafayette and head south. Today Scott and Dave opted for Falling Waters.

They set up their campsite at the Lafayette Campground as the trail literally begins right there after a quick walk through a tunnel under Rt. 93. A short walk past the parking area and into the woods where they crossed a bridge and got their legs in gear. As with the majority of trails heading out of Franconia Notch it didn't take long for things to start getting steep...real steep! Early on the footing was good and the trail almost wide enough to walk side by side. However, that changed pretty quickly as the trail narrowed and became more rocky and rooty. The guys were feeling fresh and excited to be back in the mountains and the time and effort melted away into the beauty of the picture-perfect weather and the trail.

This trail is not called Falling Waters for nothing. There are several cascades and falls almost the entire way up to the ridge. The first is Stairs Falls followed shortly after by Swiftwater Falls, and after another steep and rough climb achieves 80' high Cloudland Falls. Here they stopped for a breather and basked in the sound of the water and the feel of the sunshine through the trees. Just above Cloudland Falls they came upon a unique conjunction of two waterfalls literally facing each other as they plunged into the pool below. Dave was amazed at this sight as he had never before (or since) seen a sight that seemed so improbable: two small mountain streams, one from the north and one from the south finding the same spot hidden away in the mountains and coming together to create this lovely scene. Above this small wonder the trail continued steeply up and crossed the stream several more times. Fortunately, the water was low enough and the footing good enough and there were no difficulties. They came upon a series of welcome switchbacks to ease the climb before the trail straightened out and went right up the side of Little Haystack Mountain.

On Falling Waters Trail

Little Haystack is a misnomer. At 4,760 feet there is nothing little about it and there is no easy way to get to the summit, and anyone who climbs it deserves much credit for their effort. However, Little Haystack Mountain DOES NOT COUNT as a 4000-footer! The esoterica of the 4000 Footer Club stipulates there must be at least 200 feet of elevation change between the sag of one mountain to the next closest mountain in order to qualify for the list. The elevation change between Little Haystack and nearby Mount Lincoln does not meet that criterion so therefore, bigger brother Lincoln is an "official" 4000-footer, but poor old Little Haystack is left just to be a thorn in the side of hikers traversing the ridge. This is also the reason that Mt. Franklin in the southern Presidentials didn't qualify, as it was a "shoulder" of Mt. Monroe. Rules are rules....

From the summit of Haystack, the guys turned their sights northward up the Franconia Ridge. They had broken through the treeline shortly before summitting Haystack and the clarity of the day revealed the ridge in all its' rugged splendor and occasionally terrifying beauty. The trail stretched away before them towards the summit of Mt. Lincoln and beyond to Mt. Lafayette. They turned toward each other and let out a soft "Wow" before plunging into this picture postcard. Like a ribbon the trail went out before them towards the summit of Lincoln before disappearing on the other side and then reappearing about a mile beyond as it snaked up Lafayette. The first few tenths of a mile were inviting and nearly level before it narrowed into a near knife edge and began to ascend the rocky slope of Lincoln. Is there a stronger word for "breathtaking"? The winds were calm, and on this section of the trail they basically had the mountains to themselves, and they barely felt the exertion of the climb up to Lincolns 5,089-foot cone. Pausing for a bit and looking to the east into the vast expanse of the Pemigewasset Wilderness and the wooded hump of Owls Head below them and the Bonds beyond that gave the guys the feeling that they were alone in this world of rugged beauty. Turning to the west and the peaks of the Kinsman's and Cannon Mountain across the notch, thoughts began to stir of "We need to do those too". It was at that moment of inspiration that Scott turned to Dave and brought up the subject of the 48 four thousand footers, having recently become aware of the "challenge". In a split second, it was on! Dave heartily agreed that it was something they had to do and henceforth there would be no quitting. *Take the road less travelled.*

The Kinsmans and Cannon

Descending from Lincoln and over a few minor ups and downs the trail led to a sweet climb up to the summit of Lafayette and the broad, rocky top at 5,260 feet. It was here they ran into their first "crowd". Lafayette, although not an easy climb by any means is one of the more popular peaks in the Whites because of its 360-degree view and the proximity of the Greenleaf Hut for hikers to rest and refuel. They joined about another dozen or so hikers sharing the peak, and all agreed it was purely outstanding.

Despite Scott and Dave's newfound assertion that they were going to become Peakbaggers, they both still had a lot to learn. As with the Madison education, plus lessons learned while crossing the southern Presidentials, they were inadequately prepared in many ways for such an undertaking, and they were reminded once again on the descent off Mt. Lafayette.

They departed the Franconia Ridge Trail and began the descent from Lafayette down the Greenleaf Trail towards the hut. From the summit the hut looked so small and far away, yet it was "only" a mile, but in that one short mile they descended almost exactly 1000 feet. Walking downhill can be a wonderful thing, but do not ever for one minute think it is easy. One must watch every footfall to avoid a fall or a sprain and it's brutal on the knees, calves and thighs. By the time they reached the hut Dave's legs were howling mad at him and he suspected Scott was feeling exactly the same. They rested at the hut for a bit, refilled their water and began the homestretch down the Old Bridal Path to the campground.

There was nothing easy about it. The downward slope began almost immediately as they navigated a steep and rocky outcrop to a section of the trail "affectionately" called Agony Ridge by the hut croo. All they could think at this time, after the miles already done, is that they were thankful that they were going down, no matter how tough it felt. However, even then, they were reminded that mental preparation is just as, if not more, important than physical ability. These guys were no youngsters, and they hadn't put themselves through this level of exertion for this duration of time (over six hours) in many years. The trail continued its' punishment through a series of switchbacks before finally levelling off to an extent. Scott had fallen behind by this time, and to distract his mind from the pain Dave began simply counting his steps until he reached about 30,000 and lost count when the sounds of highway traffic made him know it was nearly over.

Meanwhile, Scott was somewhere behind and struggling more than Dave knew. Dave arrived back at the campsite and tore off his boots and rested for a while, but after about 20 minutes he was getting concerned because his hiking partner had not arrived yet. He started to walk back to the trailhead when he finally saw him coming. It was not a pretty sight. Scott was shuffling along and appeared quite wobbly, just putting one foot in front of the other. He seemed in a haze and his color was not good. They walked back to the campsite and Scott was actually shivering despite the warm summer temperature, so he sat in the vehicle with the heat on while he rehydrated. Thankfully after about half an hour he was feeling better.

This experience drove home a major point of peakbagging: along with the euphoria of a terrific summit experience, it isn't just the ascent that one must prepare for, but the agony of a rough descent as well. *When one gets to the top of any mountain, the job is only half done.*

They were so beat they really didn't even want to bother throwing together a meal, nor to sleep on the ground that night. The work was done and there was nothing left in the tank, so they broke camp and drove to Lincoln to grab a room at the Kancamagus Inn and ate greasy food at the sports bar and had a few cold beers, though they weren't really even in the mood for drinking (too much).

This trip was not only an epic across the breathtaking Franconia Ridge, but also served as the impetus for Dave and Scott to make the ironclad agreement to hike all of the forty-eight 4000 foot mountains in New Hampshire. The awesome views and the experience were truly difficult to put into words as they walked. This hike has become one of the most travelled in the entire northeast, luring hundreds of outdoor enthusiasts every week. On this terrific day, our guys learned a valuable lesson taught to many who traverse this ridge or summit any peak for that matter: the mountains tell us all that the ascent, though difficult at times is really only half the job. Different muscle combinations are required for the descent and can be very taxing on the body in a totally different manner than climbing. Six plus hours of any like physical activity is what separates hiking from many other athletic activities. Mentally, if a hiker is basking in the euphoria of a summit and the view, forgets what lies ahead on the descent is asking for a share of mental torture of sorts. *However, one must learn to love the journey as much as the destination.*

Yet, despite the difficulty, they vowed they would not be deterred and instead began looking forward to what the next trip would be. It was a successful and rewarding day overall in a beautiful place and that could not be taken away from them. But henceforth they remembered that each mountain has its own way of kicking one's ass, yet the urge to keep going never leaves once it has taken root in the soul.

Perhaps more importantly this hike, with the amazingly rugged beauty of the Franconia Ridge and the sea of the Pemigewasset Wilderness served as the force and inspiration for an almost 20 year physical and mental challenge that would change Scott and Dave's' lives.

All 48 or nothing. Lesson learned.

Franconia Ridge

Mountain Whispers

The mountains were calling
On that ridge one glorious day.
It was time to explore
Without further delay.
What lie ahead, uncertain for sure,
Time to open a brand new door.
As the journey began, goals intact
They soon discovered the skills they lacked.
Rather than doubt or concede
It was time to proceed.
Mistakes made, for sure, triumphs as well,
Part of the process, the mountains did tell.
Soon confidence replaced doubt.
They began to figure it out.

Scott Tetreault, 2022

4. Mount Carrigain

"We'll climb that hill no matter how steep."
Bob Dylan

September 2002

Although it was going to be difficult to replicate the outstanding views of the Franconia Ridge, as the summer began to wane, Dave and Scott set their focus for the next trip on Mount Carrigain at the southern end of the Pemigewasset Wilderness. They were anticipating the hike would live up to the description of the mountain, named for Phillip Carrigain, the New Hampshire Secretary of State from 1805 to 1810. Carrigain constructed a map of the entire state in 1816 and attempted to designate and name many of the mountains in the area, including some of the Presidentials.

They left Connecticut early on a beautiful September morning with a fresh attitude and growing confidence that they would accomplish their goal of summitting the 4700-foot mountain, the 13th tallest in the White Mountains. The days hike would include 3400 feet of elevation gain up the Signal Ridge Trail. *As with most things in life worth accomplishing, a positive attitude, good preparation and mental focus are always integral to the formula for success.* They were ready.

The trailhead is on Sawyer Pond Road, about 2 miles into the woods off Rt. 302. Arriving at the parking area around 10:30 AM they were a bit surprised to see a fair number of vehicles, being that Carrigain is somewhat off the beaten path than the more "popular" and accessible mountains. They really didn't think too much about it at the time as they had the usual pre-hike butterflies while loading their packs and readying themselves for what was going to be one of their longest hikes to date, approximately ten miles out and back. With that in mind they set out with the mixed feeling of anxiety and anticipation for what the mountain had in store for them.

The first couple of miles of the trail were a beautiful walk in the woods. Mostly flat and with easy grades, they soon crossed Whiteface Brook easily as the water level was low. They followed the brook for some time before they veered away and began to climb more moderately for a brief stretch. Although it was early September, Mother Nature wasn't showing her beautiful autumn colors, waiting for a few more weeks for public display. They crossed Carrigain Brook and began to ascend a bit more as they neared the base of the ridge. The trail became rockier and more difficult as it now steepened significantly up the steep valley side toward the crest of Signal Ridge at approximately 4400 feet. There were a few minor switchbacks as they got higher, making things a little bit less strenuous and after about four and a half miles they achieved the open ledge at the ridge crest. Here they decided that the first break was earned, and they relaxed with a snack and some cool water. The views from the ridge were fantastic, affording the hikers a preview of what was to come in what would hopefully be a brief push to the summit.

As the two readied themselves for the last phase of hard work, a group came up the ridge heading for the summit and stopped to say hello and comment on the beautiful weather. Interestingly to Scott, they were carrying what appeared to be poles of some sort. He assumed they may have been planning to camp in the bush that night and perhaps the poles would be used in some sort of camp setup. After a pleasant conversation the group carried on and shortly after Scott and Dave slung on their packs and continued their last push to the summit. Having crested the ridge, the walking was pretty easy as they broke into the open and gained sight of the observation tower not far above them. They passed the site of the old wardens' cabin and after one more little push up, they arrived at the summit and were surprised to see a sizeable crowd up there!

Signal Ridge

What they saw next was something they never expected. American flags were flying. A lot of them! They asked what the celebration was about and quickly learned they had unknowingly joined the very first "Flags on the 48." Up to this point neither of our hikers spent a great deal of time on the AMC websites or bulletin boards so they were unaware of this commemoration of the tragedy of September 11, 2001, almost exactly a year before today's climb.

Flags on the 48 was conceived by patriotic members of the hiking community as a way to honor the people who perished and the first responders on that awful day by having groups hike to the summits of all 48 peaks and hoist American flags on the Saturday that falls closest to the actual 9/11 date each year. It was a deeply moving experience and both men vowed they would one day participate again.

As the flags snapped in the ever present breeze of the White Mountains the two hikers scaled the observation tower to take a moment to gather in the surroundings and get a glimpse of the days rewards. According to the Guide, there are more of the 48 peaks visible from the top of Carrigain than from any other peak in the Whites. Dave didn't make the time to take out and orient the map to see how many he could identify but suffice to say the view was magnificent. After an hour or so the various groups began to dismantle their flagpoles (now Scott knew what they were carrying) and to begin their walk back down while our hikers lingered and enjoyed a leisurely lunch. After another hour they decided they needed to get moving on their own descent back to the car and to find a place to camp.

They flew down Signal Ridge like a breeze. Not only were they stronger and well hydrated, but they were also refreshed by what they had witnessed atop the peak. It was an inspiration to see that some good had arisen from the attacks and anger just a year before. This was a great example of how climbing mountains can enrich your life; *the physical health and fitness benefits are huge. Yet the mental inspiration that can be achieved is no less important.*

The walk down was as pleasant as a walk in the park, and they arrived back at Sawyer Pond Road late in the afternoon. Interestingly, by the time they got there the parking lot was deserted. The days' events, a beautiful and successful ten-mile hike with outstanding views coupled with the inspiring flag activities and the time spent at the summit did not afford them much sunlight as they approached the car. One thing was certain, they both felt they earned a few cold beers before leaving the lot. They opened the back of Scotts Volvo wagon and sat enjoying their rewards and reminiscing about the events of the day. There was a solid sense of satisfaction and feeling of accomplishment as this trip went very well, thus whetting the appetite for future trips. As was usually the case there was a bit of critiquing of their performance as they were still honing their pre-hike prep, hydration, and mental focus. However, the physical portion of this trip seemed nearly effortless with the conversation flowing freely as they experienced new adventures on the trail. Additionally, they were also learning the joy of late summer/early fall hiking with its comfortable days and brisk nights.

The decision was made to end the day with a well-deserved Mexican feast and a couple of well-deserved margaritas in nearby Bartlett. Changing from the hiking clothes and stowing their gear, they took one last sip of their brews and Scott closed the hatchback to leave. Just as the door closed his heart stopped...... the keys were in the car and the doors were all locked! It was nearing dark; they were 2 miles off the highway in the woods with no cell phone coverage late on a Saturday afternoon and they were stuck. They mulled the situation, and it became apparent there was only one thing to do besides walk out, hitch a ride, and try to find assistance. The only viable option in Scotts' mind was to smash one of the rear windows and retrieve the keys. However, he couldn't do it.... not to his nearly new Volvo. So, Dave found a large rock and heaved it at the window. One slight problem however, Volvos are built like tanks, and it took three tries including the last running start to shatter the rear passenger side window. They cleaned up the broken glass, attempted to cover the window with a trash bag and duct tape and finally with keys in hand they were on their way. The embarrassment felt by Scott was pronounced, yet fleeting, as the two turned their attention back to a memorable day in the mountains.

Despite the end of the day travails, it was becoming evident that there was a trend developing in the guys' quest for all the 48 peaks. Inspiration was beginning to replace the drudgery of physical exertion. Taking time to open all their senses, they found themselves taking in breathtaking views and being part of something special atop each mountain. The anxiety of an ascent remained but the mountains were speaking to them, often subtly.

There is so much more to hiking than just one foot in front of the other. Awe, inspiration, a joy can come from any variety of sources if one takes a moment to seek them. Stay focused to the physical aspects but look elsewhere for enjoyment. *The mountains do whisper*....... Another good lesson.

5. Mount Osceola

" Because in the end, you won't remember the time you spent working in an office or mowing the lawn. Climb that damn mountain!"
Jack Kerouac

Early Summer 2003

As spring gave way toward summer Scott and Dave turned their attention to the Waterville Valley region of the White Mountains, namely the tallest peak in the area, Mt. Osceola. Named after the great chief of the Seminole people, this mountain is one the most southern of the New Hampshire 48, and majestically stands 4340 ft, the 24th tallest of the White Mountains. Access to the trailhead is located on Tripoli Rd. near Woodstock, NH. They had spent numerous nights camping in this area years before, and the two were looking forward to a successful return. The plan was an early start from Connecticut, a 6.4-mile hike followed by an overnight at the Russell Pond Campground. This campground was located very near the trailhead; it is nestled into the hillside, with 86 nicely designed campsites, all fairly close to the beautiful Russell Pond.

Depending on how well each were feeling after summitting Mt Osceola, as well as weather conditions, time of day, etc., they would make the decision as to tackle its sister mountain, East Osceola.

The guys were continuing to learn their personal hiking strengths and weaknesses, while becoming much more proficient at planning, map reading, and physical stamina. Packs were carefully supplied with navigation aids (maps, compass, etc.), ample water and calorie laden snacks, a first aid kit, and clothing for possible inclement weather. A thorough examination of the trail description (via the White Mountain Guide), which would include time estimates, trail conditions, etc. was an integral part of the pre hike process.

An uneventful ride to the Waterville Valley area put the two in the area in good time. They decided that they would set up camp at Russell Pond prior to the hike, allowing them to easily return there after the hike. Therefore, they agreed to stop into the town of Lincoln to gather whatever supplies needed for a comfortable night of camping. Most times the two were exhausted after a day of hiking; getting everything set up prior would allow them a certain peace of mind, allowing them to totally focus on the task at hand, climbing Mt. Osceola. The two were not ashamed to admit that one their primary goals of any pre-hike ritual was to use whatever means necessary to have a cold beer waiting for them upon their descent.

After gathering necessary supplies, the two headed toward Russell Pond campground where they would choose a campsite and set up for the night. While driving toward the campground, reminiscing about their many camping adventures on Tripoli Rd, Scott soon realized that he did not have his wallet. After careful examination of what could have happened, he soon came to the conclusion that he left it on the roof of his vehicle when gassing up and must have fallen off on the drive over. After frantically searching the vehicle, Scott and Dave began a thorough search of the roads recently driven upon, in a hopeful attempt to locate the missing wallet, to no avail. Scott called his wife and explained to her what had happened, so she could report lost credit cards and perform whatever other duties necessary.

Mountain Whispers

After giving up on their search (which took a couple of hours), Scott and Dave turned their attention to the hike; although the later start would preclude summitting East Osceola, they set off on the Mt. Osceola trail on what was still a beautiful day in New Hampshire to achieve the goal of the day. As they gathered their gear and loaded their packs in anticipation of the hike the usual butterflies were settling in as expected. The trail begins as a flat and smooth amble through the hardwoods; it soon becomes much rougher and littered with rocks that were nearly impossible to step over or around. Careful attention to each step was a burdensome necessity that soon became quite tedious. Neither needed an ankle sprain, knee injury or an embarrassing fall. Soon the trail conditions improved, and the two were enjoying a fairly moderate climb with better than average footing. One of the highlights of the Mt Osceola trail was its use of numerous switchbacks; a switchback can be defined as a "part of a trail that cuts sharply from one direction to another while going up a steep mountainside." Instead of climbing straight up to the summit, this specific trail characteristic allows a hiker to expend less effort and eases the hikers burden while ascending.

Soon the guys found themselves in much more open areas, hiking along flat ledges offering them beautiful views of the Waterville Valley region. Shortly after they found themselves on arguably one of the most beautiful mountain tops in the White Mountains. The sky was mostly clear and there were excellent views in all directions, including the Sandwich Range and the Tripyramids, a future goal for the two. Both were feeling strong after the ascent, however the time taking in the scenery was short lived; bug season was in full force, and both were swarmed with black flies. Not having properly prepared for this (although one could argue that there is not much that can be done to fend off such an onslaught), they decided that moving, i.e., descending the mountain, would be the most prudent choice of action. On this trip, and for the first time, Dave brought his iPod nano; soon he was off, listening to his favorite tunes, and doing what he did best, scampering down a mountainside. Throughout all of their hiking adventures, Dave was the most proficient at hiking down any mountain. He arrived at the trailhead, adrenaline pumping, music blasting, in just over an hour. An amazing time for sure, although he had to wait a bit for a cold, celebratory beer as Scott had the keys to the vehicle. Scott stayed fairly close but did slow down a bit in the rougher, more rock laden parts of the trail. Soon the two were sitting in comfortable chairs, boots off and enjoying a well-deserved beverage of their choice. The mood of the day became a bit more subdued as thoughts then turned to Scotts' lost wallet.

The day was winding down, but not to be deterred from a great night of camping, the two returned to the campsite. After a few more cocktails, and a wonderful dinner of hot dogs, beans, and potato salad, the two tired hikers sat in front of a roaring fire, totally content with all the day's activities. Soon, however, they were both startled by a voice in the dark, calling out Scott's name. After Scott replied to the voice, which turned out to be the campground host, it was discovered that she had his lost wallet! Apparently, it didn't fall off the roof of the car on the drive over, but when he did a three-point turn near the campsite. What a turn of events. Relieved and overjoyed, the life-long friends sat by the fire, somewhat amazed how this day turned out. An overwhelming sense of accomplishment for yet another positive experience in the White Mountains. This is a small testament to the types of people who hike or tend to the campsites: *when one is in the wilderness, there are good people around you who will help at any turn.*

There were times during their quest for the New Hampshire 48, that both Scott and Dave felt that there was some sort of external force surrounding them on their adventures, looking out for them, and keeping them safe. Neither could really explain what or who it was, but it seemed real. As you will see in future, it seemed to keep happening.

What's next?

Mt Osceola Summit

6. Mount Jefferson

*"Mountains have a way to make us seem small in all the
right ways"*
Sir Edmund Hillary

July 2003

After their very successful trip up Mt. Osceola, (despite the wallet
fiasco) the men turned their sights back to the Presidential Range for the
next challenge and decided to attempt the third highest peak in the White
Mountains, 5712-foot Mount Jefferson. Scott's son Mike would be joining
them once again to show off the strength and arrogance of youth and to set
a pace that would make a roadrunner winded. The trip from Connecticut
began early once again as they enjoyed the chatter and coffee as they
made their way northbound on a lovely, but warm July morning.

Instead of attempting the route to the summit from the Pinkham Notch
area through the Great Gulf, they instead decided that their highway to the
peak would be the Randolph side of the mountain via Lowes Path. That
trail, cut in 1875-1876, is the oldest to ascend the peaks of the northern

Presidentials from Randolph Valley. They parked at the roadside relic of Lowes Store, paid their nominal fee and with the usual pre-hike jitters loaded the packs, finished the coffees, and set off into the woods across Rt. 2. Crossing the accoutrements of modern life, a snowmobile trail, the Presidential Range Rail Trail and some power lines, they soon found themselves becoming wrapped in the silence of the trail.

What started out in Connecticut as a warm July morning was developing into a hot day in the mountains and it wasn't long before they had broken into a solid sweat. There was some concern as to if they had brought enough water, but none were about to turn around and go back to the store for more bottles and added weight to the packs. This area, as is common with areas under the purview of the Randolph Mountain Club, is crisscrossed with many paths and one must pay extra attention to the signage while hiking to ensure not straying off on any other path than the intended one. The first couple of miles climb only gradually while crossing the Link Trail and past the divergence of the King Ravine Trail, where things begin to get rougher and more steep. They passed the cutoff to the Log Cabin shelter and shortly after that also crossed the Randolph Path. From here, things got harder.... much harder. They came upon a section with some serious boulders and had to watch their steps to avoid turning an ankle or slipping and smashing a knee. They slowly made their way to the crest of the ridge and were pleased to see the path offered a little break. The trees were starting to thin as they climbed, and they could see the clouds were dropping and that they would soon be enveloped in the thickening fog. Reaching the Gray Knob Path, they turned left and took the short walk to the Gray Knob Hut, run by the RMC, to take a breather, have a drink and towel off the sweat.

The Randolph Mountain Club huts do not offer the "glamping" experience that the AMC huts do in the sense that there is not a full time "croo" on hand and you don't get served a delicious meal at the end of your long hiking day nor a hearty breakfast the next morning to fuel you. For your (very reasonable) fee, you get a piece of floor (maybe a mattress on the floor) to sleep on, access to a kitchen facility to prepare your own meals and a table or two to sit at to eat and play cards. However, if one doesn't like the crowds of the AMC huts, the RMC version offers a quiet, sheltered place during a mountain journey. This would be the accommodation for the evening.

On the trail to Jefferson

A general rule of thumb is that if you are ascending about 1000 feet per mile then it can be comfortably said that a trail is considered steep and often difficult. The guys had been walking just a shade over three miles to Gray Knob and a referral to the Guide confirmed their hunch that they had ascended almost exactly three thousand feet. Digging further, Dave calculated they had a little over two miles to go to reach Jeffersons summit with about another 1500 feet of climbing. This was not going to be easy. They dropped their packs at the hut to lighten the load and set out.

It was a bit after noontime, but the fog was so thick by now it seemed much later. As they ascended above the tree line there was some disappointment that any kind of decent view today was not going to happen; the visibility was less than 50 feet. The plan out of the hut was to take the Gray Knob Trail about a mile and a half to the junction with the

Gulfside Trail at Edmands Col and then the Loop Trail to Jeffersons summit, a distance they figured would take an hour and half to two hours. However, as mentioned previously, this area is crisscrossed with many other trails and somehow, they zigged onto the Perch Path when they should have zagged to stay on the Gray Knob Trail. It was pretty level, so it didn't seem like a big deal when they came to the Perch Shelter, but then they did the same damned thing again and continued on the Emerald Trail! Still not really realizing they were diverging away from the intended itinerary they found themselves descending at a pretty steep pitch for about another half hour until they came across a sign informing them they were at the junction with the Castle Ravine Trail. This was not a great development and it led to a lot of questioning of themselves and their navigational abilities, particularly when they referred back to the map and discovered what was ahead of them to get back on track. They found they were about a mile off track to get to the Gulfside Trail, but in that distance they had given themselves another thousand feet of elevation to conquer. They were not pleased, and this drove home the fact that *overconfidence and not paying strict attention has consequences.* Fortunately, they discovered their error reasonably quickly and got back on track.

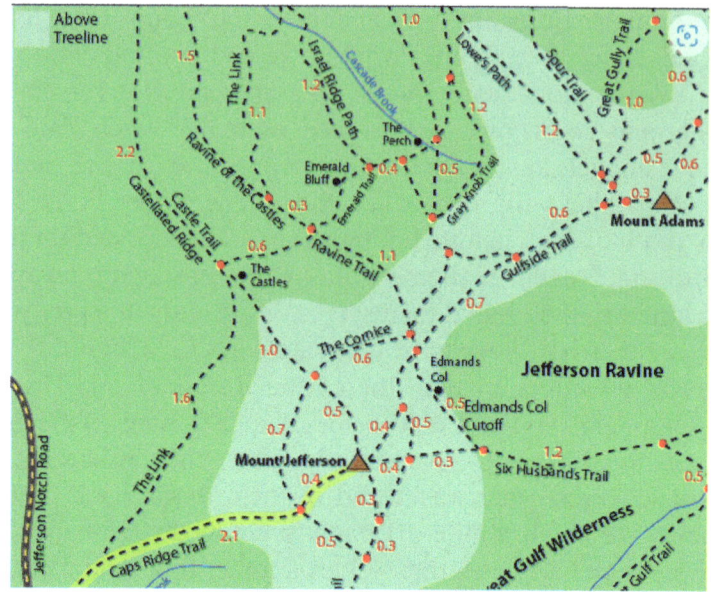

Crisscrossed with trails!

They soldiered on and up, but Scott was beginning to feel the wear of the extra climbing as well as the mistakes made, and his enthusiasm was waning. It may have been better if there was some scenery to look at once they broke through the tree line (again), but the fog was so thick when one looked around it felt as though they were inside a ping-pong ball. Eyes were focused on the footing and the trail and they were not about to make another miscue. Finally, after bouldering and scrambling and huffing and puffing and bitching they came upon the Gulfside Trail…a good two hours later than anticipated.

From Edmands Col they covered the short distance to the Loop and took a quick break. Scott was spent and informed the other two that he was not going to make the last push up the summit cone to the peak. Mike and Dave tried to urge him to join them for the lousy four tenths to the top but he was having none of it. He would wait for their return.

Mike and Dave set off in the gloom and reached the peak in pretty short order, though they really didn't feel much like celebrating. The wind had picked up a bit and the fog was swirling. Visibility was nil as they hunkered down against a boulder for a quick drink and a protein bar and a congratulatory handshake. They sat there for maybe ten minutes before descending back for the rendezvous with Scott.

By the time they rejoined him he was feeling better and had used the time to really pore over the map so the trip back to Gray Knob would not be as mismanaged as the trip to Jefferson. With Scott leading the way, they made their way back to the Gray Knob Trail and actually stuck with it the whole way back to the welcome site of the hut. They got inside, shed their boots and relaxed as darkness began to fall over the mountains. It wasn't long before the caretaker arrived and they had a nice talk with him about the days efforts and he concurred that the RMC trails can be pretty confusing, particularly when the weather isn't the clearest. If nothing else, it offered a bit of consolation to the crew about their wrong turns. They paid their fee, asked a few questions about the use of the facilities and he was soon gone. It appeared that they were going to have the hut to themselves this night as darkness had fallen and no one else had arrived, so they set about whipping up a little dinner of some freeze-dried meals, which after the day's efforts were as gourmet tasting as any dinner served in a five-star restaurant. For the evening entertainment, it was going to be playing pitch by candlelight and sharing a small flask of bourbon that Scott had slipped into his pack. Bedtime came early as they sacked out in the second floor loft on what felt like the most comfortable mattresses ever.

Morning dawned early and they were up before sunrise for instant coffee and granola bars, and they were packed and out the door by seven AM. This time there was no question or debate as to where they were headed: straight back down Lowes Path for the three miles to the car and the mad dash to Lincoln for the huge breakfast they were craving. Finally, this time the trip down was uneventful, no keys locked in the car, no lost wallet, no issues as they made their way to eggs, pancakes, bacon, and real coffee.

There was no intention of driving straight home, so they decided to do some exploring and maybe an easy (no peak) hike. A drive across the

Kanc seemed a good way to while away a couple of hours and they did the touristy thing of stopping at the overlooks to stretch the weary legs and enjoy the warm sunshine. They made their way to Sabbaday Falls, and though quite crowded they took a short walk and cooled their feet in the chilling water. These falls were carved out several thousand years ago by the receding glaciers of the last ice age. There are actually two waterfalls with a glacial bowl of amazingly clear water. They used to swim there years ago but sadly was now prohibited and that squashed the desire to plunge in. Is that progress? They hung around for about an hour before hitting the road and heading towards the North Conway area where they killed a little time and bought some beer for the evening before heading north to Pinkham Notch.

For the uninitiated, Pinkham Notch is the hub of almost all the activity that goes on around Mount Washington. (Not to take anything away from the Crawford Notch side of the mountain of course!). It is the jumping off point for many trips up Washington through Tuckerman's Ravine as well as a great place for a meal and lodging. They browsed the shop, looked closely at the 3D rendering of the Presidential Range to get a bird's eye view of what had been accomplished the previous day, took a sobering look at the list on the wall of the many people who have perished on Washington over the years, and lounged on the porch for a bit watching the comings and goings of many hikers and tourists. It was a great way to spend the afternoon.

It was at this point in Dave and Scotts hiking endeavors that they decided that a camping experience needed to be included each time they hiked in the White Mountains. They had both been avid campers for years and always enjoyed a night or two in the wilderness. However, checking the forecast had not yet become a part of their pre-hike routine. They arrived at Dolly Copp Campground, a wonderful place with an interesting history that they wanted to reacquaint themselves with, particularly because they had many hikes ahead in the Mount Washington area. They arrived at Dolly Copp as darkness fell and set up their tents by car headlights. At this time, they only had small tents and little camping equipment besides a couple of folding chairs, so it didn't take long to set up. They had eaten earlier at the "World Famous" Mr. Pizza in Gorham, so the plan was to set up, get the fire going and have a few beers.

Great campground!

However, the weather turned on them. As is typical in this area, on this night the weather took a quick turn for the worse. Just as they completed their setup the skies opened up and they found themselves in the midst of a two-hour downpour! They tried desperately to give themselves some shelter by gathering some long sticks and a tarp and whatever rain gear they had. Keeping as dry as they could they huddled under the flimsy cover, enduring the storm and toughing it out while keeping the fire burning. Eventually the skies cleared, and they were able to enjoy a beautiful night under the stars smack dab in the heart of the Presidential Range. Another one of those experiences not to be forgotten.

7. Webster-Jackson Loop

"In the mountains there are only two grades: you can either do it, or you can't."
Rusty Baille

Spring 2004

After finishing 2003 with the trek to Mt. Jefferson's summit, Scott thought the southern Presidentials required a bit more attention. At the extreme end of the Presidential range in Crawford Notch sits Mount Jackson and he was calling their names. Often this peak is coupled with nearby mount Webster to make a sweet loop using the Webster Cliff Trail and they couldn't resist the lure of conquering two summits, even if only one was a 4000-footer.

Contrary to what many believe, Mount Jackson is not named for President Andrew Jackson; rather it is named for the 19th century New Hampshire State Geologist Charles Jackson. However, as one might expect, Mount Webster is indeed named for Daniel Webster, the 19th century politician and unsuccessful Presidential candidate. Go figure.

Getting their usual early start from Connecticut and properly fueling up with coffee and breakfast sandwiches on the way, Dave and Scott arrived at the Willey House Station around mid-morning and when they got to the trailhead were a bit surprised to find it nearly deserted. To them this was not a problem: they always enjoyed the company and camaraderie of their fellow hikers and respected them for their perseverance and spirit of adventure, but these guys also loved the solitude of the trail. They decided to tackle the loop clockwise to ensure getting 4052-foot Mt. Jackson at the very least, and if they found they were too spent they could bail on 3910-foot Mt. Webster, not that they had any intentions of such a move. Gearing up and double checking who had what items, such as map, guidebook, first-aid kit, etc. they set off with a bit of the usual trepidation but feeling really good on the cool, calm, sunny morning.

On the ride north Dave suggested that once they hit the trail to take a short detour to the Elephants Head Overlook. They hit the trail, entered the woods and a short tenth of a mile later diverged onto the Elephant Head Spur and headed up a steep knob before falling back to the ledgy outcrop and some tremendous views of Crawford Notch. Anxious to get back on the trail in pursuit of the day's goals, they stayed only a few moments before zipping back to the trail and resuming the trek. The trail for the first mile and a half showed a lot of love; that is, several sections of nearly flat walking punctuated by steep uphill pitches. Pretty quickly they came upon another side path to Bugle Cliff, and Scott really wanted to see it. The day was young, and they were fresh, so they took the short jaunt over to the massive outcropping and another spectacular view of the Notch. They took a few moments for a snack and a drink and to savor the view before heading back to the main trail and knew very shortly they would arrive at the branch to lead them up to Jackson.

The trail ascended easily for a bit, then got a little steeper until they came upon a small stream, they had to cross three times. Dave was muttering to himself, "Is this really necessary?", but he didn't build the trail; he knew he was a mere traveler taking advantage of someone else's long ago labor there would be no complaints! In another half-mile or so they found themselves at the base of the steep climb up the rocky cone and ledges to the summit. In short order, not without some serious huffing and puffing and cursing they found themselves on the open summit after a great 2.6 mile walk. *Mountains teach us awareness of breath.*

It was roughly mid-day and a perfect opportunity for a peak top lunch. They dropped the packs and were enjoying some fruit and PB&J bagels when literally out of the clear blue they found they had a guest. A nosy guest, a hungry and persistent grey jay who was not going to take no for an answer. This was obviously not his first rodeo with hikers up here; he inched closer and closer, cocked his head sideways as if to say "Welllll?" Who were they to say no? They tore off bits of the bagel and handed them over as closely as the jay would allow, but he would not take them from one's hand. Jay etiquette, perhaps? But the second the goodies were placed on the rock he would snatch them up, fly to a nearby bush, enjoy his treat and then be right back for more. It was a great way to spend lunch with a new companion. These little unexpected occurrences are what often are the most memorable on any given trip. Scott and Dave were having a great time and Mr. Jay came along to enhance it even more. *Savor the little moments that you are given, because the best things in life are often unexpected and usually free.*

From here they departed the Webster-Jackson Trail and left the summit to head to Webster on the Webster Cliff Trail, which is a short section of the Appalachian Trail. To Dave, it always felt good to be walking any section of the AT after his aborted trip many years earlier. Though he was never able to be a "Thru-hiker" or "End to Ender", it somehow seemed as though he was coming back to an earlier quest. They headed generally southwest toward Webster.

The walk to Webster was a piece of cake. They descended the cone of Jackson, carefully picking their steps and soon found themselves on a nice, nearly flat, although very boggy stretch of the trail. Thank God for the work of the trail crews: All through this area were built plank walkways that not only made the walk very pleasurable but also protected the environment and plants in this area. It wasn't long before they came upon a drier section signaling the short and easy climb to the summit of Webster. Within just a few minutes the two found themselves once again high above Crawford Notch looking down at the ribbon of Rt. 302 and the peaks of the Willey Range to the west. These men always counted the views as one of their rewards for their efforts, and this one certainly did not disappoint. Lingering on the summit and soaking in the sun and feeling of accomplishment, the siren song of a few cold beers in the cooler sitting in Scott's car began to dance around their minds.

Still feeling pretty fresh they attacked the descent off the rocks of Webster but were soon slowed by several areas of really rough and wet footing. It wasn't super steep, but like the Jackson Branch of the trail, never relented too much until it intersected with that branch and rejoined the main section of the trail. It was actually a bit of an eye-opener as they did not anticipate the walk off Webster would be so taxing on the knees and quads. Regardless, they made good time and enjoyed the level sections of the trail between the drops and soon found themselves back at the trailhead and the parking area.

Webster-Jackson Signage

In no time, the boots were off, the chairs were set up and Dave Matthews Band was playing as they settled in to quaff a few well-deserved beers. Dave had brought along another little post-hike treat that would soon become part of each post-hike ritual: a small propane grill to cook up some hot dogs. A few dogs with relish, onions and mustard and frosty cold beer henceforth would become part of almost every celebration of completing another peak. At one point a truck swung by and the driver, obviously a hiker himself, stopped and said, "Boy, you guys really know how to live!" He got no arguments. As they sat enjoying yet another beautiful day in the White Mountains their thoughts turned to the next challenge. The day spent on Mount Jackson and Mount Webster was a positive experience for both Dave and Scott. The mountains offered up some beautiful views of Crawford Notch, historic Crawford Path and the southern Presidentials, yet with less physical exertion than previous trips thus far. For the first time the trails taken offered up an opportunity to explore a mountain not on their list. *Take a new path, find a new experience.* A lesson that would stay with them as they continued towards their goal. One more 4000-footer in the books.

8. North Twin, South Twin, and Galehead

"I took a walk in the woods and came out taller than the trees."
Henry David Thoreau

October 2004

Next up on the list was an attempt at summitting three mountains, North Twin, South Twin, and Galehead. The men decided that a day in mid-October would not only afford them some beautiful mountain views but some remaining fall foliage as well. This would be their second attempt at hiking three peaks in a single day, being that when they did the southern Presidentials they skirted around Eisenhower on the first day and grabbed it on day two on the way back south. Reservations were made at the Galehead Hut for another enjoyable night of good food and good hiking company after the days' work was completed. This was the last night the hut would be open as they close down for the season in mid-October.

They drove up the day before and arrived in Lincoln as the day was waning and spent a comfortable night at the Kancamagus Inn. A great breakfast at Brittany's Pub was the lead into a beautiful day weather-wise in the mountains, with a little nip in the air and wall to wall sunshine, perfect hiking weather. Their confidence was growing with each endeavor, and they were comfortable not only with the plan of the day but also their ability to accomplish the goals they had before them.

With the usual caffeine induced butterflies in their stomachs and full packs the two started out on the North Twin Trail fairly early in the morning. The trailhead is about two miles deep in the woods off Rt. 3 and begins by following an old railroad grade, making a nice easy way to begin the journey. Both men agreed that it is always great to start a trail with some nice and easy walking, allowing for a warmup period without the grind of steep ascents right off the bat. It allows time to get the muscles warmed up, get acclimated to the weather and the trail conditions as well as to get a feel for how the day would progress.

Pretty quickly into the walk they came to the first of three stream crossings of the Little River. According to the White Mountains Guide these crossings can be difficult during periods of high water, but this time of the year the water is typically low, and the bottoms of their hiking shoes barely got wet. The trail ascended moderately for about three miles before, as expected, it got really steep, and they slowed their pace to meet the demands ahead. Not stopping at this early point in the climb they pushed on and achieved a beautiful outlook to get the first reward for the efforts thus far. As stated earlier, they were becoming more competent in their hiking abilities and thus far today were moving quickly and with relative ease. The 4,760-foot summit of North Twin was reached in about two hours and forty-five minutes, having completed the 4.3 miles well ahead of expectations. They stayed atop North Twin only long enough for a snack before heading towards South Twin, the second goal of the day. The North Twin Spur to South Twin is an easy 1.3 mile relatively flat walk that to Dave was reminiscent of the stretch they had done earlier in the season between Jackson and Webster peaks. In no time at all they were on the open ledges of the 4,902-foot peak. The combination of the weather, the views played out before them of the vastness of the Pemigewasset Wilderness, and the satisfaction of having completed two peaks before noontime made the day a success already. Both hikers were feeling strong, invigorated, and looking forward to the rest of the day.

From the top of South Twin could be seen the Galehead Hut below, a relatively small speck almost lost in the scenery. To get to the hut they would continue on the Twinway with an extremely steep descent to get there. The conversation turned to how difficult this was going to be to climb back up tomorrow morning as they continued down the trail over a series of rock "stairs" and arrived at the hut in less than an hour.

The Galehead Hut is a beautiful, albeit somewhat smaller AMC facility nestled between surrounding peaks on the edge of the Pemi at an elevation of 3,780 feet and is considered one of the most remote huts in the White Mountains. Scott and Dave sat on the porch for a while, enjoying lunch and taking in the views, while congratulating themselves on what they had already accomplished on the day, although they knew there was still more work to be done. After registering with the croo, dropping the packs, and selecting the bunks, they made their way toward completing goal number three for the day; Galehead Mountain, approximately a measly half-mile away. Literally within a few minutes they were atop the 4,024-foot peak which offered no views at all from the treed summit. Having been spoiled with great views thus far all day, the guys spent almost no time at all and headed back to the hut to enjoy the rest of the afternoon.

Front porch sittin'

Upon returning they enjoyed more porch time and let the feeling sink in; three peaks on a gorgeous October day. As they sat and chatted with others, they learned the hut was only going to be about one-third full this evening, due to the fact it was late in the season and the hut was closing. They did observe a few of the seasoned hikers carrying and enjoying an early "beverage of choice" that they carried up with them in light containers, and once again chastised themselves for missing the mark and musing about how great a celebratory cocktail would be. This was a lesson learned that would not be forgotten!

After a great pasta dinner, brownies for dessert, and some excellent conversation with the hut-mates, they turned in for a well-deserved nights' sleep. Due to the fact the hut was not full, Scott and Dave had the small bunkroom to themselves, a rare occurrence, so Scott only had to listen to Dave's loud snoring all night instead of a room full of tired hikers. Despite that annoyance, it was actually so quiet, the hut so secluded, and everyone so respectful of the others' nights, sleep was comfortable and peaceful.

Awakened at 7:00 AM feeling fully refreshed and rested and anticipating another lovely day in the mountains they packed their things and marched out to breakfast. As always, the croo put out an excellent and fortifying meal while updating the weather and trail conditions and instilling a positive and upbeat attitude for the day. About 8:00 they said their farewells to the hut and embarked on the return trip beginning with the one arduous mile hike back up to South Twin. One thousand plus feet in one mile. Throughout the remainder of their hikes, Scott would always use this standard to determine the degree of difficulty of any hike. Looking up, it seemed so long and steep and both guys were feeling the stiffness of the prior days' work and not really looking forward to it at all. One foot in front of the other up the Twinway they climbed, deep in the heart of the Pemigewasset Wilderness. Scott was feeling strong, and he left Dave in the dust pretty quickly, yet about an hour later they were both once again sitting atop South Twin gazing across the wilderness at the Bonds, a future goal. They knew that all the "heavy lifting" for the day was already done.

When one pauses, stops to look around and breathes, things sink in. *With each hiking adventure you learn. You learn about yourself. You learn about your hiking partner, your gear, and so much more. You learn what you've got in you. Your capabilities and stamina. Your desire to push yourself beyond some preconceived notion or idea of what you are or what you can do. The mountains do that to you.*

Occasionally you learn from other hikers. On this day our two had a nice conversation with a couple on top of South Twin who informed them that their plans were to continue across the Twinway to the Bonds and eventually all the way to their vehicle located at the Wilderness Center on the Kancamagus Highway. Wait? What? How far are you going? It seemed so overwhelming to Dave and Scott to comprehend how far this young couple intended to go. While the older guys were feeling pretty good about themselves, they were scratching their heads at the ambition of the other's plans. It left a deep impression on them and led to setting more difficult goals for future trips. Looking back, it became evident that the youngsters' plans were not so crazy; they were young and in shape and full of the spirit that drives one in these mountains. Over time our guys met several people who had completed full Pemi or Presi traverses and though ambitious or even daunting, longer hikes began to be worked into their plans too. This couple helped open their eyes wider.

53

Turning north on the spur, in short order the two guys were back on North Twin and ready to commence the descent back to the truck. Yet before they started down, they had a moment to stop and pause and experience one of those moments that never leaves a person. No, it wasn't the weather, or the tremendous views; not this time. They stopped and found themselves enveloped in silence. A silence so "loud" it seemed deafening. Not a whisper of wind nor the rustle of a leaf. Not a plane and certainly no road noise. They stood and watched a hawk gliding lazy circles in the sky above, drifting in the quiet. Mother Nature at her finest. Nothing to say. Shut up and soak it in. Try to think of the last time you were enveloped in total silence. *Enjoy the small things. Embrace the silence.*

Dropping off the summit they breezed through the four miles or so and returned to the truck with a huge sense of satisfaction and accomplishment at having finished three peaks, another enjoyable AMC hut stay and some unforgettable experiences. Thoughts and feeling that would carry them for the remainder of their times hiking in these White Mountains. As is the case so many times, *a day in the mountains is food for the soul.* The feeling of being away, enjoying the natural world, breathing fresh, clean air, and pushing ones' physical and mental abilities is like no other.

What's   next?   Can't   wait!

9. Mount Adams

"Today is your day! Your mountain is waiting. So, get on your way!"
Dr. Seuss

Summer 2005

The summer of 2005 was dragging on into late June when Scott turned to Dave and said "Enough!" and they headed to the solace and peace of the mountains again. Still dancing around the northern Presidentials, they had to get Mount Adams done to wrap up the 4000 footers in that area. The Randolph Mountain Club maintains so many trails and paths in that area that the guys had a myriad of options to choose from to make the ascent. Because they had a great walk up Lowes Path when attacking Jefferson, as well as a really nice night at the RMC Gray Knob Hut they decided to follow that route again with one notable change: they would instead try out the Crag Camp for the evening's accommodations. After a successful '04 there was excitement about 2005 and the possibilities it offered. Confidence was growing, equipment being added or improved; Dave added a new and better pair of hiking shoes, as well as some good hiking pants and dry-fit shirts, while Scott brought a lighter pack and a better small cookstove into the mix. Anticipation was high, so why not tackle the second tallest of the Whites, Mount Adams, standing at 5,774 feet amongst its brothers in this rugged range? They had been crossing off the Presidentials mostly one at a time believing it would be best to get the biggest and hardest out of the way first while filtering in some of the smaller peaks. One thought was certain: this trek would cover 4.7 miles one-way and offer 4,550 feet of elevation gain. They understood this was not going to be a breeze.

The reason Crag Camp was chosen for the nights' accommodations this time was the location: clinging to the high edge overlooking King Ravine and promising a magnificent view. There was a spring nearby and the kitchen facilities were available to them, so rather than doing an "up and down" the thought of staying the night was a comfort. Additionally, the older guys would once again be hiking with Scotts' son Mike and nephew Marc and the Crag Camp option offered a great opportunity to socialize with a couple of young men after what promised to be a pretty tough day.

They had another somewhat uncomfortable night getting rained at Dolly Copp Campground, but it didn't dampen the spirits as all awoke early the next day chomping at the bit to get going. They headed for the trailhead only after stopping in Gorham for a "hearty" McDonalds breakfast and coffee to fuel the fire. They arrived at Lowes Store around 8:00 AM, paid the modest fee, bought a couple of snacks, loaded the packs, and set off for a long day in the woods. It was a nice, clear day although at the trailhead it was hot and muggy from the prior nights rain. Over the years it seemed that they had this tendency to hike in hotter weather, possibly waiting for school to get out or to avoid buggy season as best they could.

As expected, the trail begins rather tamely, meandering through the woods at easy grades. This time they knew to pay close very attention to the intended route due to the many paths that intersect with Lowes Path, and they didn't need another wrong turn to add to the mileage or elevation they knew they were going to face ahead. After about a mile and a half the trail does begin to steepen and get rougher after a few small brook crossings. There was some concern circulating as to whether the group had brought along enough water for the ascent on this hot day. It was hot, the sweat was pouring off all of them and the trail was getting steep, however, everyone seemed fresh as they pushed up this beast of a hill with the views getting sweeter as they made a push up to Norwell Ridge. After 3.2 miles and approximately 3000 feet of elevation gain, they arrived at the junction of the Gray Knob Trail where the plan was to follow it past Gray Knob to Crag Camp for a short rest, some rehydration, and a snack before pushing on.

It's hard to explain, but the mentally grueling "sport" of peakbagging actually makes one feel so much better at these moments. When the first goal has been reached and the ultimate goal of the day is clearly within reach. You feel tired. You can feel the aches that will haunt you later after the day is complete. You feel the nagging bit of doubt that pervades through endeavors such as this, feeling that for one reason or another you may fail. *Determination is what pushes you on. While Perseverance makes the goal and knows that You. Will. Not. Be. Deterred. It is during times like that where you muster your strength and feel the will building in you to believe you can accomplish anything you set out to do.* These are some of the lessons learned in the mountains.

Arriving at Crag Camp, the gang met the caretaker, paid their fee and selected their mattresses for the night. Refilling the water bottles at the spring nearby, gobbling down a PB&J and a change of shirts goes a long way towards reviving one for the next step. They still had work to do. The sun was shining brightly as they left the hut lighter and refreshed for the roughly mile and a half remaining with a ton of elevation gain still to come. They turned up the Spur Path to rejoin Lowes Path and encountered one of those moments on the trail that always sticks in ones' memory, snow in the middle of June! They found themselves walking through a snowfield remaining from the winter on a hot day in the White Mountains. It should have been expected, but even so they were taken aback a bit. Continuing to push on towards the steep and rocky cone of Adams, the fatigue was beginning to be felt building in the legs of the older guys and they distracted themselves by thinking and talking about the nice meal they would enjoy tonight hanging out at the hut and relaxing after a good days' climb.

One thing that was certain is that the trail was offering superior views in all directions. The summit would be attained soon as each guy was silently putting the pedal down to finish this ascent, knowing the views from the top would be sublime. In short order they reached the 5,774-foot summit after one more laborious push up the path. And stretched out, 360 degrees around them were some of the most spectacular views on the White Mountains. Madison to the north, Jefferson just to the south and Clay behind it. Looming above all beyond Clay was the hulk of Washington. The Great Gulf Wilderness expanse to the east and King Ravine plunging to the west. Stunning was not a strong enough word as they stood in silence.

As they savored the view and their accomplishment, they found they weren't alone on the peak. Not by a long shot. In fact, there were thousands of others joining them. Biting flies descended upon them like a Biblical plague! When they arrived at the summit there was a pretty stiff breeze blowing so they didn't really notice them at first beyond being a slight nuisance, but when the wind subsided these monsters came up from the rocks and were having a field day feasting on every square inch of exposed flesh. All directions, all extremities, they attacked relentlessly and tormented each man trying to slap them away without success. Not even taking the time for a quick snack they bailed off the summit and returned to the trail within ten minutes unfortunately. Needless to say, they likely set personal speed records for the descent off Adams as they desperately tried to escape the onslaught of the voracious pests.

After slowing a bit when they escaped the pest plague, they returned to the hut later in the afternoon knowing they had another great day of hiking in the Whites with the boys. The heavy lifting of the day was done, the views over and down into King Ravine were outstanding and made up for not being really able to savor the view from the summit for long. A nice supper was prepared, a huge batch of pasta and sauce, bread and whatever else may have been available in the packs. Scott oversaw the kitchen once again as he had brought some preboiled rigatoni and a bag of his wife's world-famous sauce and he didn't disappoint as they all packed on the calories they had burned throughout the day.

Mike, Scott, Mark and Dave after Adams

Full bellies intact, the remainder of the daylight hours were spent playing rummy with the boys and having fun, thoroughly enjoying the time and the peace of Crag Camp. Interestingly however, a discovery was made as they played: Apparently, there has never, ever been anyone as bad at the game of Rummy than Marc!! Despite all the coaching, teasing, and ball-busting he just could not seem to grasp the concept of three of a kind, or a run, or what to discard…. Epic card ineptitude, and he was not spared the jabs of his cousin and his uncles. However, let it be said clearly that on the trail, both younger men showed the elders how to do it: physically fit and willing to accept any challenge the trail would present.

Most of the trips together found Dave and Scott well behind them although they never took any unnecessary risks or strayed off the trail.

After a sound night's sleep, coffee was made pretty early the next morning as they took in the views again. Awakening high in the mountains is one of those special pleasures that must be earned, and the reward is sweet. No traffic sounds, no news screaming at you, no special agenda or timetable or job to have to run off to. They whipped up some oatmeal and munched on a few Cliff Bars, refilled the water and loaded the packs to head out. A pretty slow and leisurely descent took them back to the car by about noontime. The sun was shining, they were feeling good and were famished once again. Mountains make one hungry. They drove off to Gorham and revisited Mr. Pizza and gorged themselves on appetizers and two large pizzas with the works. Wholesome(?) food for hungry hikers and they knew they would be back again one day soon.

Reflecting on the trip on the way home, Dave mentioned to Scott he had a gnawing tinge of regret. They were certainly getting better at this stuff, the planning, the physical and mental performance, and more. Yet it was beginning to seem they were so laser focused on bagging any given peak they were missing something else. There is so much to explore in the White Mountain National Forest and all too often the side trails and waterfalls and other vistas get overlooked or pushed aside in the blind push to add another peak to one's list. A simple days climb to a hut and some exploring of a gem like King Ravine would be a great day of activity. This had to be considered, yet there was so much more work to do.

Looking towards Mt. Madison from Adams summit

Being single minded towards achieving a goal is an admirable thing. However, there are times when one needs to pause and take in the beauty around   *them.*

10. Mount Tom and Mount Field

"In life, it's not where you go, it's who you travel with."
Charles Schultz

June 2006

As 2005 drew to a close, Scott and Dave looked askance at each other and expressed disappointment at the weak effort they had put out for the year. Yes, they did have a very successful climb of Mount Adams to complete summitting all the major peaks of the Presidential Range, but that was it! They had bigger plans, but life kept getting in the way and that precluded them getting north any more than that one trip. They vowed as the year turned that they were damned well going to have to do better if they ever wanted to complete the 48 peaks and join the 4000 Footer Club. They decided that they needed to get more "multiple peak" trips into the agenda and start making a serious dent in the list. Up to this point they had completed 15 peaks: a bit shy of a third of the goal. At 50 years old the clock was ticking, and they weren't getting any younger.

There was still a lot of work to be done in Crawford Notch, so they chose an early June day to tackle two of the "smaller" 4000 footers, Mount Tom and Mount Field, and if they felt really good, perhaps scoot over and grab Mount Willey while they were in the neighborhood. These peaks are all part of the Willey Range, a steep ridge that rises out of Crawford Notch, and despite the summits all being just a bit over 4000 feet, they are by no means an easy trek. The beautiful part is that once the ridge is crested the walking is pretty easy and undulates between the wide summits and the cols in between. But in order to enjoy this one must pay their dues to get there.

This day would just be the two hikers, as anyone else invited had other obligations, so an early departure from Connecticut got them beyond the traffic and to Lincoln early enough for breakfast before they drove across the Kanc to Bear Notch Road, which would lead them to the Notch and the trailhead at the Highland Center. The Avalon Trail was chosen as the initial route up the ridge, and for the first several hundred yards was a nice way to wake up the legs with easy to moderate grades. They crossed Crawford Brook a couple of times with no issues as the water was low and continued quickly to the intersection with the A-Z Trail. Turning right and continuing the ascent on A-Z they were quickly reminded once again that almost any trail that climbs out of a notch is going to get very steep very quickly and both the Avalon and A-Z trail held true to that adage. It got steep, rocky and rooty for a solid mile and turned out to be a pain in the ass (and legs) to push their way to the junction with the Willey Range Trail. Being that they were on their first summit trek of the season after a not-so-ambitious winter, Dave was griping about his legs being sore and being pretty winded. He suggested to Scott they make the short jaunt to grab Mount Tom and take a break. The blackflies surprisingly weren't too bad yet, so it sounded like a good opportunity to sit and reconnoiter for a bit. They got to the 4,051-foot summit after a solid 2.8 mile walk in a little less than two hours. While enjoying a light snack, Dave began to get the feeling that there were eyes on them. Glancing around he didn't see any critters like a squirrel or a mouse and shook off the feeling until he heard a flutter nearby. Turning to his left he once again found they had a new friend in another hungry gray jay. The bird cocked his head at Dave as though to say, "Hey! I'm hungry!", and not being able to resist the birds persistence, the two guys shared lunch with him. Soon enough he was joined by another partner in crime and both fowl enjoyed bits of sandwich and trail mix. This went on for about a half hour as the men enjoyed the incessant begging as the jays took the goodies off to stash them somewhere nearby and then hurriedly came back for more. It was a nice diversion from the early aches and pains of the walk thus far as they loaded up for the trip over to Mt. Field.

Grey Jay

A short walk back to the trail and a quick zigzag had them rejoin the Willey Range Trail for the mile over to Field. What a beautiful walk it was. The punishment of the A-Z Trail was over, and this was a simple, easy undulating walk over to the summit of Field at 4,285 feet. They were enjoying their accomplishment once again as they looked south over to Willey, about a mile and a half from where they stood. They looked at each other as though to question whether to go for it or not, and a simple mutual shrug made the decision. Similar to when they climbed Mount Osceola and stared over to East Peak a short distance away, they turned away from Willey knowing they would be back another day. Honestly, it was an error; they should have gotten it right then and there as the route

64

they chose upon their return trip would prove to be much more arduous. More on that later.

As they began the descent Dave offered to Scott that at the very least, they owed it to themselves to take a little detour down the Avalon Trail and grab the summit of Mount Avalon. It seemed like a small consolation prize for their laziness at not getting Willey. The walk was moderately steep, and they made good time over the roots and rocks and were atop Avalon in short order. Mt. Avalon may be shorter in stature compared to its neighbors but it more than makes up for that by offering beautiful views the others do not. Although it is not a treeless peak, there are outlooks at some of the rocky ledges to the east and the Presidential Range that are as good as any in the White Mountains. Looking down into Crawford Notch and the ribbon of Rt. 302 winding its way through the greening valley on this June day was inspiring. Another gray jay popped by and got a few tidbits for a moment before they pressed onward and downward.

From here the trail got steep again with some rocky scrambles to negotiate carefully. Being they were pretty fatigued, and the burn was rising in the legs they took their time as the work of the day was nearly complete. The A-Z Trail came back in to their left as they turned right and headed back towards the Highland Center for the rewards waiting in an ice-filled cooler. As they hustled down the trail, they mused that this two peak trip was a success and if they wanted to really make a dent in the list, they needed more trips like this.

Arriving back at the trailhead, the boots were shed, the chairs put out and they cracked a few frosty cold ones and cooked up some delicious hot dogs. Daves' legs were screaming at him, and he could tell that if indeed they were going to do more trips like this it might be time to add in another piece of new gear into the arsenal. He had never really given much thought to using trekking poles prior to this, but the more he thought of it, particularly considering his habit of bouncing down trails with some sort of reckless abandon, poles made sense. Up to this point he had not had any falls but thinking back to his AT days and the damage he did to his knees back then he was questioning himself as to why he didn't have the common sense to start using poles earlier. A shopping trip was in order before the next journey. *Every mountain will teach you at least one important lesson. Whether they teach you to bring rain gear or better shoes, or in this case that trekking poles can be a valuable addition, you learn something every time.*

They enjoyed their beers before packing up and heading off to Jigger Johnson Campground over on the Kanc. Arriving before dark gave the opportunity to set the tent, to make some dinner and relax as darkness fell as they "turned on the TV" (that is, lit the fire for the evening entertainment) and discussed the successes of the day and pondered what would be next on the list.

Scott   mentioned   the   Bonds….   Hmmmm….

11. Zealand Mountain, Mount Bond, Bondcliff, and West Bond

"Without mountains, we might find ourselves relieved that we can avoid the pain of the ascent, but we will forever miss the thrill of the summit."
Craig D. Lounsbrough

August 2006

Summer 2006 was wearing on and the itch grew stronger to get back to the mountains and get busy once again. The guys had been talking about the Bonds since their trip up Mts. Tom and Field and they decided it was time to go big or go home. They had been keeping in shape with some pretty strenuous hikes around their area and were feeling strong and confident. On some of their recent local hikes they had been joined by another friend who was curious about their treks and expressed interest in joining them. Russ was another life-long friend and former athlete like Dave and Scott, and he wanted to push himself into a new level of activity and he was warmly welcomed to join the next journey. He used to be the fullback on their high school football team and one time in a close game he actually carried two opposing players on his back into the end zone to score the winning touchdown in a close game. He had the legs of a climber, huge calves and thick thighs and at that moment earned the nickname of "Tree Trunks." It was time to put those tree trunks back to work.

They chose a weekend in late August to make this trip as they figured they would be well beyond bug season, and they wouldn't have to carry too much in the line of clothing in the warm weather. Up to this point, their trips had typically been two-day escapes: drive up, grab the intended peak, camp and go home. On this trip they wanted to stay in the woods longer, so they decided to get up there, take the Zealand Trail to the Zealand Hut to spend the night, grab the planned peaks the next day and then spend the night at the Guyot Shelter before hiking back out on the third day. They were fired up as they headed north again and enjoyed filling in Rusty on some of the earlier adventures as well as what he should expect over the next few days.

In no rush on Day 1, they took their leisurely time getting up to Lincoln, grabbed a bite to eat, stopped at the Mountain Wanderer shop and bought some tee-shirts before heading out across the Kancamagus once again. A quick zip across Bear Notch Road to Rt. 302 found them back in the familiar terrain of Crawford Notch where Scott pointed out to Rusty the peaks he and Dave had already done. Unfortunately, the clouds were lowering, and it appeared there would be rain coming in soon. As they turned down Zealand Road the fears came to fruition as the skies opened and they found themselves at the trailhead in a downpour. Not an auspicious beginning as they sat in the car for a while and waited for the rain to let up. After about 20 minutes things seemed to ease a bit and they decided it was now or never to get moving to the hut.

Into the woods on the Zealand Trail, the group was in high spirits and anxious to get some miles under their feet as the rain picked back up once again. Despite their growing sogginess it was evident the Zealand Trail was one of the most beautiful trails in the White Mountain National Forest. It starts off easily by following an old logging railroad bed allowing the legs time to loosen up as it climbs and descends moderately over some small ledge areas and a couple of stream crossings. Soon they came upon an open area of beaver bogs which the trail crosses on zig-zagging boardwalks, allowing some glimpses into Zealand Notch as they strained to catch sight of a beaver. Shortly beyond that they re-entered the woods on a sweet, flat walk that took them past Zealand Pond where the beginning of the Twinway joined to lead them up to the hut. The rain was steady by now and they all were anxious to reach the first goal of the weekend to relax and dry out.

However, the Twinway was about to provide them with an eye-opener. It wasn't far to the hut, but it was a steep son of a gun and it made them pay for the ease in which they had gotten to that point so far today. They climbed a series of rock steps upward, carefully watching the footfalls as the rocks were wet and could be slick. In the distance could be heard Zealand Falls roaring from the days rains and they picked up the pace to go see it. It was a torrent crashing down the rock faces of the ledges and they dare not get too close as one wrong step would have been a serious blunder. From here it was just a few minutes until they stood on the porch of the hut, feeling relieved being out of the rain.

Roaring Zealand Falls

Checking in, they were assigned a bunkroom and commenced trying to fish some dry clothes from the wet packs. On the way up, Dave was thinking of investing in a pack cover, and it was at this moment he realized how valuable they could be as almost everything was at some level of dampness. Throwing on a pair of quick drying shorts and a dry-fit tee shirt he and the others commenced to finding every hook, post, and chair they could to hang the rest of the clothing to dry. Although the walk up to the hut was a short one (about an hour and a half), they had managed to work up a pretty good sweat in the humid rain and the bunk space quickly took on the scent of a locker room. It was getting later in the afternoon when the three guys joined a group of fellow hikers in the main room for some lemonade and a snack while the croo was prepping what promised to be a great dinner in the galley. Because of the relative ease of reaching this hut, it was pleasing to see there were a couple of families with younger children there for the night too. Scott mentioned how great it is to see mothers and fathers taking their kids to the mountains and showing them the joy of being "away" from everything. Keep in mind, this was in the era before the proliferation of cell phones with the capabilities they have now, and through all the guys' journeys they never saw anyone with their face buried in a phone, texting, playing a game, tweeting, or insta-facing (whatever). As usual, the meal was hearty and good and camaraderie strong amongst the croo and hikers. The guys sat on the porch for a while and watched the sky clear into a beautiful sunset before retiring and getting rest for what promised to be a long and strenuous next day. Back to the bunkroom, and though the air was tinged with "Essence of Sweaty Feet" they fell into a sound sleep.

Early next morning they were roused by the sweet sound of a flute playing in the hallway to announce that breakfast would be served in about 30 minutes. They wasted no time in repacking the still damp clothing and getting stoked for the coming day. Breakfast was blueberry pancakes, fresh fruit, and strong coffee to fuel the fires. They ate, did their personal business and were out the door by 8:00 AM or so and back on the Twinway. Not 50 feet out of the hut the trail began to climb again, although not as steeply as it did when climbing to the hut the day before. The legs were getting into working order when they came to an offshoot of the trail leading to Zeacliff, a spectacular overlook down into and across Zealand Notch. As far as the eye could see, clear blue sky, the lush greenery of the notch, and Dave made it a point to mention to the guys that there was not a single, solitary sign of mankind to be seen. Not a road, not a railroad, not a cell tower, nothing. Clean air, forest beauty and silence were the rule of the morning. As they sat taking it all in, they were joined by a member of the hut croo. She told them that today was her day off and she was heading out for a "little" 24-mile hike today! Scott shook his head in amazement and admiration of these young folks who think nothing of hauling 75 pounds of food up to the hut on a wooden frame one day, then just for the fun of it go out and hike a 20 plus miler the next. This young lady also taught Dave another lesson that he uses to this day: as they sat and chatted, she took out a couple of Tylenol and popped them to ward off the pain she knew would be coming sometime. Dave had always taken something after a hike was done but it never dawned on him to take something before to keep the pain at bay. Henceforth, he always carried a bottle of pain relief with him.

They soon split up as the croo member headed down the steepness of the Zeacliff Trail and the guys carried on towards their first goal of the day, Mount Zealand. The footing and trail were good, and they had only one "obstacle", that being one steep section with a ladder to climb before the path basically levelled out. In less than an hour they took a small side path leading to the summit of Zealand; a non-descript cairn in the middle of a small clearing. They kind of shrugged their shoulders at the underwhelming scene, but Scott and Dave checked another one off their list! For Rusty, this was his first 4000-footer besides Mount Washington many years prior, and it was evident there was pride, but also a certain sense of disappointment in his eyes at this particular peak almost as though to say, "This is what you guys have been raving about?" The other two knew he was in for some eye-opening stuff soon enough.

Zealand Notch from Zeacliff

All three beelined back to the Twinway and resumed heading for the Bonds by losing some elevation into some deep and misty woods before climbing once again towards the wide, rounded summit of Mount Guyot ahead. Scott and Dave were feeling strong and soon found themselves nearing the top of Guyot, but they had lost sight of Russ. They weren't worried about him as they knew he was as strong as an ox and would be coming along soon enough. Earlier there was mention of Russ's earlier in life nickname. Well, Mr. Tree Trunks is one of those guys who never quits. He came back into view shortly and though not moving quickly, he was moving steadily and with determination. He was not going to be defeated. Dave and Scott watched him from atop 4,580-foot Mount Guyot and lamented once again that there they were, atop a 4000-foot mountain that DOESN'T COUNT as there isn't the required elevation change in regard to the nearby peaks. Technicalities for sure, but rules are rules.

Rejoined with their other hiking partner, they dropped of Guyot and soon split off the Twinway and joined the Bondcliff Trail for the easy walk over to the path leading to their accommodations for the night, the Guyot Shelter. Taking the spur path leading down to the shelter they made their reservations for the night, claimed spots in the lean-to and dropped the majority of their gear. Heading back to the rocky climb back to the main trail, Dave was now appreciating his latest addition to his gear list: he was now using a pair of trekking poles that he had purchased a few weeks back after doing Mts. Tom and Field. He bought them primarily for stability when descending slopes and trails in his typically rapid descent off mountains, but this section of trail also taught the value of being able to use upper body strength when climbing as well. Not only are they a great aid in helping one lift oneself up a slope, but he also discovered that his hands didn't swell as they used to when at his sides on previous climbs. They remained a valuable and welcome addition for the rest of his climbing career.

Rejoining the Bondcliff Trail they covered the easy stretch over to Mount Bond in good time and found what they had expected, a look out over the vast emptiness of the Pemigewasset Wilderness. Now Rusty could see what the others had been talking about and as he sat on a boulder eating some trail mix he commented on how this view made all the effort worthwhile. Scott reminded him there was still more work to be done as he pointed over to the southeast at Bondcliff, the next goal. Rusty seemed rejuvenated with the view and was ready to roll almost immediately.

They headed down off the summit of Bond into the steep descent and the scrubby trees, picking up their pace to get to where they would break out of the woods again along the ridge leading to the overlook. As they broke through, they were greeted with a potentially ominous sight: there were storm clouds building to the west and the prevailing wind was in their faces, meaning it was headed their way in all likelihood. They hustled to the cliff and stood on the incredible overlook into the Pemi Wilderness: the peaks of Franconia Ridge across the way, the spire of South Twin to the north, and Owls Head nestled in the forest below. Easily one of the most awe-inspiring views in the White Mountains. However, they knew they shouldn't stay on the exposed ridge for long with summer storms heading directly at them and they turned to go back up Mount Bond.

It was here something interesting happened. By now the guys were starting to feel the fatigue and none of them were too excited about having to go back up that rugged slope. The wind was picking up quickly at their backs as they walked. Knowing they were in at least some minimal danger Scott mentioned the wind assisting them as we moved along. There was no lightning to be seen or thunder to be heard as they pushed up the slope so that eased their minds a bit, but both guys mentioned to Rusty it was the only time either ever truly felt a wind-aided push up a slope to get them to relative safety. They did get pelted by some rain for a bit, but the expected storm thankfully never materialized. They made the summit of Bond and without hesitation scooted over to grab the last goal of the day, West Bond.

Bond Cliff

At this time Russ was feeling pretty spent and not being on the "quest", opted to bypass West Bond and head back to the shelter to relax. The other two tried to cajole him to make the short trip but he was having none of it and headed off. Dave and Scott jumped onto the spur path and found themselves climbing steeply and steadily towards the 4,540-foot peak. They made the summit in only 15 minutes and, although better than the summit of Zealand, West Bond offered little in the way of a view or anything worth lingering over. Back down to the main trail for the jaunt down to the shelter and a welcomed rest.

By now they were learning the ropes of making their evenings after a hard days work much more pleasurable. They rolled out our bags, threw the hiking shoes over in the corner to air out and relaxed as other hikers made their way in. It was then they met Old Goat, an AT Thru-Hiker. Over the time and trails Scott and Dave spent in the mountains, surprisingly they had not met, to their knowledge, any thru hikers, so it was a pleasure to chat with him about his adventures and travails on the AT. Old Goat was about their age, from upstate New York and had been on the trail for several months. He showed the wear and tear in both appearance and his clothing. Scott asked what in his opinion was the toughest section of the entire AT he had done so far, and he said without hesitation the White Mountains of New Hampshire were the most consistently rugged he had crossed. He was looking forward to Maine and reaching the summit of Mt. Katahdin but was also wary of what he expected to be rough work getting there through the Maine mountains and woods. Though Dave wrote him several months later, he never heard back from him again and can only think that his perseverance and determination got him to the top of Katahdin and the end of his 2000 mile walk.

While chatting, Scott fired up his pocket rocket stove and made some freeze-dried something or other that tasted way better than it should have, filled up their water at the spring, washed the days grime off a bit and relaxed. As the sun set, they dug into the "evening pleasure": a flask of bourbon and some fine cigars that Scott had squirrelled away in his pack. Sitting there with feet dangling over the edge of the elevated shelter and letting the ease of a mountain evening seep in. Old Goat muttered as he drifted off to sleep something about "You guys really know how to live", and at that moment all they could do was agree. Sleep came early and easily.

The shelter began to stir before daybreak, and they dragged themselves awake to begin the return walk to civilization. A quick protein bar for breakfast, some early hydration, and a trip to the outhouse and ready to go. They set off with Old Goat up the spur trail and back over Mt Guyot, and it became obvious that this guy was truly a mountain goat after all his months on the trail. He left our hikers in the dust within the first couple of miles and was gone. It was early in the day, and nobody was in a rush, having achieved the goals of summiting Zealand, West Bond, Mt Bond, and Bondcliff. They made their way back to the Zealand Hut for a quick rest and water refill and headed back to the Zealand Trail, over the boardwalks and to the car. As was now the usual custom, they set up their chairs and dug deeply into the cooler (which still had ice) and fished out a few frosty cold ones to celebrate while Dave grilled up some dogs. Having had done about 20 miles over the few days, and though to many it may not seem like a lot, to these guys, and to Russ in particular it was a great accomplishment. Personally, Dave knew he was going to pay for it with a few days of his tired legs rebelling at every staircase encounter, but this was a feeling that would not be traded for all the creature comforts of civilization. Russ vowed he would be joining them for more trips in the future and he was assured he would always be welcomed.

One of the few regrets they shared about this trip was not being able to spend more time on the edges of Bondcliff and enjoying the camaraderie and the stunning view. The weather was turning potentially nasty, and it caused them to hustle back to grab West Bond and to the shelter earlier than planned because the expanse of trail over to Bondcliff is exposed and potentially dangerous in storms. *Unnecessary risks are not an option.*

The group departed for Connecticut satisfied with their work and knowing there were still several good months left in the year to grab another peak or three. Where would the focus fall next?

12. North and South Kinsman

*"There are moments when all anxiety and stated toil are
becalmed in the infinite leisure and repose of nature."*
Henry David Thoreau

September 2006

Following their epic trip to the Bonds, Scott and Dave decided to
complete a great year of hiking with a September trip to Franconia Notch.
They opted to hike North and South Kinsman. The Kinsmans, along with
Cannon Mountain to the north, make up the spine of the Cannon Kinsman
Range and offer great hiking with fantastic views of Franconia Notch and
well beyond. The plan was an approximately 10-mile day, leaving from
their campsite in Lafayette campground. The two left Connecticut on a
beautiful autumn day and arrived at the campsite around 9 AM. After
choosing a campsite near the trail, Scott and Dave quickly set up their
tents, looking forward to a superb day in the woods. They took the
Lonesome Lake trail right out of the campground, and it started off
relatively easy and meandered through the notch, arriving at the beautiful
Lonesome Lake after just 1.2 miles. The lake provides hikers with a
spectacular clearing, affording magnificent views of Cannon

Mountain, the three notable Cannonballs and Mt Lafayette across the way. Tempted to remain lakeside gazing at the views, the guys knew they still had work to be done as they soon arrived at the popular Lonesome Lake Hut. The days were certainly getting shorter and the two had a relatively late start, so off they went to accomplish what they had set out to do, summitting 2 peaks.

Leaving the hut, they soon found themselves on the Fishing Jimmy Trail in the midst of a steep, rough 2 mile climb with about 1200 feet of elevation gain that would lead to Kinsman Junction. This trail was named for a well-known resident of Franconia named James Whitcher. It begins rather tamely, crossing a few brooks before becoming a bit more moderate and perhaps lulling the pair into a false sense of complacency. However, the trail is cut directly over several ridges and the result is a series of "PUDs", described as pointless ups and downs. One major peeve about ascending on any trail is to lose elevation while in the throes of a steep climb. Extra elevation gain is never a welcome sight and can take its toll on the mental outlook of any hiker if not prepared. Soon they found themselves at a series of wooden steps mounted in the side of ledges to assist hikers up another steep section of the trail. The trail became rather muddy at this point and soon after another brief ascent Scott and Dave found themselves at the scenic Kinsman Pond. After taking the beauty of this mountain pond, as well as the adjoining tent site, the two turned their attention to the summits looming across the pond.

Happy to be off the Fishing Jimmy Trail, they set out to complete the task at hand, but things soon took a turn for the worse. The two made a key navigation error; not paying attention to the map, they inadvertently took the Kinsman Pond Trail instead of heading up the Kinsman Ridge Trail. Heading in the wrong direction for almost a half an hour, hiking in blissful ignorance, Dave came first to the conclusion that they were not gaining elevation and that the pond should be on the left of them as they traversed the area. Time to take out the map. A bit angry, and quite embarrassed, they immediately turned back unhappily, and reacquainted themselves with the proper direction and soon they found themselves at the junction of the Kinsman Ridge Trail. Hiking in the White Mountains often keeps one humble; sometimes it is the weather, sometimes equipment, other times physical stamina. This time was a repeat of some past mistakes, and neither was too happy about it. On a positive note, however, the mistake resulted in what would best be described as "angry hiking." With a quickened pace, and more determined than ever, Scott and Dave were on the summit of North Kinsman feeling much better about each other and the day as a whole. The summit of 4293-foot North Kinsman is wooded and the two found a nice overlook and rested with a snack, and a sense of accomplishment.

Sensing that the day was winding down, the two set off for the second goal of the day and quickly navigated their way across a .9-mile ridge walk to South Kinsman. When they arrived on the second summit of the day, they were rewarded with another fantastic view on the open summit. To the east was the indescribable Franconia Ridge, North was Cannon Mountain and the Cannonballs, and to the west was the beautiful Mt. Moosilauke. Despite getting misplaced a bit on the ascent, both Scott and Dave were feeling very good about the day's efforts, having garnered two more peaks and being treated to some very scenic views.

By now it was late afternoon, and the day was winding down, and it was time for the descent. Both were feeling physically and mentally strong; as usual Dave set a mean pace and glided down the mountain listening to music, bouncing off the rocks with agility and speed. Scott was not far behind him, content with his pace. Soon, as darkness began to set in, the two were together again for the last mile, and arrived at the campsite feeling quite good about the hike, although a little sore in the legs. Nothing a cold beer and a great meal by the fire couldn't cure. The temperature had dropped significantly; after a change of clothes, a couple of steaks, and numerous liquid refreshments Scott and Dave found a roaring fire to be not only warming, but extremely relaxing as the two debriefed the days activities. Tired muscles were forgotten. All in all, a very good day in the mountains, two more peaks, lessons learned again and a strong sense of personal satisfaction.

Ironically the two hikers had only spent 12 hours in the mountains, but it felt like they had been away for a week. They would return home in the morning, refreshed, and with a positive mental outlook that can only be garnered in the wilderness. The lessons learned from their many experiences in the mountains will remain with them for a lifetime. The feeling that they carried within this time, was that *a day or two in the mountains is one of the most rewarding and relaxing ways to escape the stresses of day-to-day life. You return with a renewed, yet humble sense of mental health that prepares you for things that may arise in your daily existence.* A nice finish to a great year of hiking.

13. Mount Willey

"Sometimes you will never know the value of a moment until it becomes a memory."
Dr. Seuss

Spring 2007

The year 2006 had been a fantastic year for Scott and Dave in their quest to "bag" all the 48 four thousand footers in the White Mountains. Probably one of their best in terms of the number of peaks bagged, the beauty of those mountains, and the invaluable experiences they were gathering; bottom line, they were more accomplished hikers and that meant they looked to 2007 with great expectations.

As part of the winter long discussions about future plans and preparations, they decided that they would attempt back-to-back climbs, that is, one peak the first day and another on the next, an endeavor that had never been attempted by the two. Growing confidence, and a desire to "push the envelope" a bit, their attention turned to Mt. Willey, a 4285-foot peak in the scenic Crawford Notch State Park. It is named after Samuel

Willey, Jr, a resident of Crawford Notch whose family perished in an avalanche in August of 1826. It is part of the Willey range and ranks 29th in elevation of all the 48.

As mentioned prior, the trip's itinerary evolved after numerous discussions over the winter; day 1 would include an ascent of Mt Willey and day 2 would be Mt. Hale. These two mountains were relatively close to each other and were 2 of the smaller peaks in the White Mountains. Scott and Dave had regrets about not having bagged Mt Willey in 2006 when they opted not to include it during the hike up Mt. Field and Mt. Tom. Many times, decisions are made out on the trail and are made with many factors in mind, including fatigue, time of day and weather conditions. Summitting Mt Willey would clean up this minor matter and would, with Mt. Hale, complete all peaks in the Crawford Notch area for both guys. Completing Mt. Hale would also complete another goal of theirs, back-to-back days of hiking. Many hikers do this all the time; Scott and Dave wanted to use this opportunity to become better hikers, improving both mental and physical stamina. Always looking to get better.

Day one's plan was to attack Mt. Willey from the south side, including the Kedron Flume Trail, briefly on to the Ethan Pond Trail and finally the last 1.6 mile push up this mountain. Driving up from Connecticut, the two arrived at Willey House trailhead about mid-morning, geared up and hit the trail immediately. The Kedron Flume trail began rather easily, wandering through the woods and began to climb via a series of switchbacks. Soon it reached a beautiful waterfall of the Kedron Brook at which time the two took a short break. From there the trail followed a small brook and got much steeper and rougher until it eased as it approached the Ethan Pond Trail. After a tiny bit of time on the Ethan Pond Trail, they soon found themselves in the "meat" of the hike, as the Mt. Willey trail soon turned rough and steep. Scott and Dave were continuing to believe that each four thousand footer has its difficult sections and usually manifested in different ways for sure. Soon the two found themselves climbing a series of wooden ladders, attached right into the ledges of the trail, similar to what they found on the Fishin' Jimmy

Trail. These "stairs" are rough and steep and sometimes slippery, and provide no safety railing, or anything in general to clutch onto. A hiker must pay very close attention ascending each stair; final count was 96 steps overall, each assisting the hiker through a very steep section of granite. It was slow going and tough, but they could only imagine how much tougher it would have been without the trail crew's dedicated hard work.

The Ladders

Scott and Dave soon found themselves at the summit of Mt Willey, overlooking the beauty of Crawford Notch, and north across the southern Presidentials. Dropping their packs, they found themselves enjoying the scenic views, and chomping on a banana, an orange, and some trail mix.   The conversation turned to *a sense of gratitude toward those individuals who maintain the numerous trails throughout the White Mountains. Without them hiking would be nearly intolerable. Every tool, every slab of wood is hauled up these steep trails. It's work not for the faint of heart, but these rugged maintenance men and women keep the trails safe and passable for hikers of all abilities.*

The two soon put their gear back on, and began their descent, feeling strong, and looking forward to the challenge. Dave put The Band on his headset, leaving Scott in the dust, busting his quads, carefully watching each step. Soon the two found themselves at the wooden stairs, and decided to do this in unison, as these stairs were a bit more ominous on the way down. Keeping an eye on each other was something they had grown so accustomed to, having become nearly second nature.

After safely climbing down through this very steep section, they could again begin to make time and hustled toward the parking lot. Dave arrived at the vehicle first in very good time but had to wait for Scott to open the car for a cold beer. As was the tradition, take off the boots, grab a chair and crack a cold one. Nothing better. The talk of the days activities turned to plans for tomorrow's hike up Mt Hale.

Off to Jigger Johnson campground for a nice meal, cozy fire, and a comfortable   nights   sleep.   More   to   do   in   the   morning.

14. Mount Hale

*"You don't have to be a fantastic hero to do certain things.
You can be just an ordinary chap, sufficiently motivated to
reach challenging goals."*
Sir Edmund Hillary

Spring 2007

Fresh after a successful hike of Mt Willey, and after a restful night of sleep, Scott and Dave awoke ready, willing, and motivated to tackle Mt. Hale. The legs were surely a bit tired and somewhat sore, but the morning weather on the Kancamagus was outstanding. No excuses today. After a breakfast of oatmeal and a bagel, the two prepared for the hike, packing the usual items and mentally envisioning the hike. All systems were go including a few of the normal pre hike butterflies, much of those caused by Scotts high octane coffee.

As mentioned earlier, these guys had never attempted back-to-back hikes on their quest; many serious hikers do this routinely, and the two thought it high time that they attempted such a task. The choice of climbing Mt Hale was also figured into this day, as it is one of the easiest hikes of any 4,000 footer. A 4.4-mile round trip up the Hale Brook Trail to the summit with approximately 2270 feet of elevation gain. A more moderate hike on day 2 was the final decision, not knowing fully what to expect of their legs and physical stamina in general.

Arriving at the trailhead around 9am, sun shining, the air clear, the day began on a positive note. It was calculated the out and back would take roughly three to three and a half hours depending on how long they lingered on the summit. Stiffness and soreness soon abated as they made their way across a bridge, then to the initial crossing of Hale Brook. The water was very low at the time so an easy rock hop across found them in a more moderate climb through the woods. They crossed the Hale Brook a second time, then the trail soon climbs away from it, the rustling stream no longer to be heard. The flow of any stream while hiking is always a welcome sight not only for its natural beauty, but for the soothing sounds it lends any hiker, allowing a mental escape of the monotony of a climb. Eventually the trail grade eased a bit and it traversed through a beautiful stand of birch trees. Soon the trail steepened and ascended via a switchback or two, for what would be the last push to the top. To this point there only had been slight views of the surrounding area, and Scott and the Dave wasted no time getting to the summit in excellent time.

The summit of Mt Hale is a surprisingly large clearing on the rounded top surrounded by large conifers that had grown over the years; it is the sight of a former fire tower; however, it had been torn down and the surrounding trees had all grown to a point where there was literally no view of any kind. Although they expected this, it was nonetheless disappointing to both. There is a huge cairn on the summit of Hale, which is impressive, but views are always the ultimate reward for any ascent.

Mt. Hale summit

Not to be distracted, both Scott and Dave put on their headphones and took off on what they both felt would be a rapid descent off at Hale. Dave took off in usual fashion, setting the pace, with Scott close behind. Legs were feeling good on day 2, trail conditions perfect, all contributing to making this hike almost a run down the mountain.

In just a little over an hour they crossed the snowmobile trail that told them the parking area was mere moments away. It wasn't long before the pair found themselves at the car, happy with results of the days' activities, and enjoying a few cold beverages and debriefing the events of the past 48 hours. Two peaks in two days. Feeling good, getting closer and closer to the goal of all 48 peaks. More importantly, a growing sense of confidence in their hiking abilities, ready to tackle whatever the White Mountains threw at them.

Despite the disappointment of the views on the top of Mt Hale, it was still a positive experience in many ways. Just being in the mountains, hiking with a friend, accomplishing a two-day goal, and finally *CHALLENGING oneself! That's a recipe for a great day anytime, anywhere.* Even if was "only" Mt Hale.

15. Mount Garfield

"Nature teaches more than she preaches"
John Burroughs

Mid-Summer 2007

An opportunity arose in late July that seemed too perfect to let slide by: Scott's son Mike was home from the Air Force Academy and was really feeling the itch to get back up into the White Mountains while at the same time his nephew Marc found himself with a few free days. The three were sitting on Scott's deck one shining afternoon when Dave joined them and naturally the discussion turned to which peak this group wanted to conquer. The two younger men were open to almost anything which allowed Scott and Dave to make the decision to tackle Mt. Garfield. However, to make it more interesting for the crew, the choice was made to turn this into an adventure and make the trip from the summit of Garfield back across the Franconia Ridge and revisit Mts Lafayette and Lincoln and then spend the night at the Liberty Springs Tentsite. Marc and Mike were all in and within a couple of days the crew was underway northbound.

As this trip was not a loop or an out-and-back, it was going to require two vehicles and car spotting; that is leaving one vehicle at the end of the trail and then driving to the trailhead, so as they usually did on the trail the two younger men took off from Connecticut early and left Scott and Dave in the dust as they wended their way to the Lafayette Campground as the rendezvous point. Gear was quickly loaded into the starting vehicle while the other was left at the trailhead near the Flume Gorge parking lot and soon the group found themselves at the Garfield trailhead and ready to go by 8:00 AM.

Starting Up

Since this was going to involve an overnight stay at Liberty Springs full packs were the order to accommodate sleeping bags, tents, cooking supplies and food and a thorough check was made to ensure they had all they would require. By 8:30 the boots hit the trail. The plan was for the first rendezvous point to be the summit of Garfield. Fortunately, the younger men carried most of the weight.

Typically, the two younger studs were soon out of site as they took advantage of the easy grade the trail follows as it traces the path of an old tractor road that once led to the summit fire tower. The two older gents chuckled as they wished they still had the strength to keep up with the younger generation but did not complain because they were back in the environment they loved as they walked together for the first couple of miles. However, it wasn't long before Scott once again outpaced Dave on the ascent and both hikers carried on their solo climb.

The walking was easy as the trail climbed slowly through beautiful woods, a couple of stream crossings, and soon enters an area of pines and a series of wide switchbacks up the moderate slope. It was in this area that Dave decided to take a short break for a snack and a few swallows of water and to enjoy the silence of the forest. A quick granola bar and a guzzle of half a bottle of water and ready to go. Then a setback: slinging his pack on, Dave felt his back wrench and seize up!! It had been years since he had any back problems, but he knew this was not a good thing and the pain increased as the lower back muscles spasmed. He looked around and listened; not a sound and no one to be seen. Real thoughts began to enter his mind as he faced the dilemma of trying to carry onward or to abort and go back to the car. One problem; he didn't have the keys for the car! This was in the pre-cell phone era so there was no way to contact any of his fellow hikers to tell them what was happening. Dave contemplated turning around and returning to the trailhead but with no way to let anyone know it was inevitable the crew's trip would be ruined if he didn't show up on top of Garfield. Hoping the pain would ease if he kept moving, he made the choice to carry on.

There was only about another mile and a half or two miles to the summit and the walking ahead looked easy, so he soldiered on and slowly, carefully resumed the trek. The strides weren't as long, and the pace was significantly slower, but it wasn't too long before he got to the last rocky and steep pitch up the summit cone and managed to scramble up the ledges to the site of the foundation of the summit tower on the wide-open peak. He rejoined the crew waiting and having lunch and slid off his pack and laid down on a flat slab to try to stretch out the angry muscles. It wasn't pretty and involved a lot of grunting and groaning.

The rest of the crew was in fine shape and ready to press on, but they lingered for a while as Dave rested. Not wanting to make anyone quit on this lovely sun splashed day Dave told them to go on and he would meet them on top of Lafayette. They stuck around long enough to make sure he got his pack on and were somewhat convinced he could make the next leg of the journey before they all departed together.

Scott stuck with Dave for the steep descent off the rocky cone of Garfield but was soon out of sight as the two continued their walk alone through the sag between Garfield and Lafayette on the Garfield Ridge Trail. This particular stretch of the trail, though lovely and fairly easy, is made more of a pain because as it crosses several ridges along the slopes of each mountain there are numerous PUDS! That is, "Pointless Ups and Downs" which make for more work ascending; climb one ridge and then seemingly lose half the elevation only to climb another and then lose elevation again. Scott and Dave had come across this phenomenon before, most notably on the Fishin' Jimmy Trail so it was not foreign but didn't make it any easier or less frustrating. The good news was that torment only lasted for a couple of miles until the next tease began. As the Garfield Ridge Trail ascends Mt Lafayette, even though the woods get a little thinner and the views open up, the fact is that one can't really see the summit of Lafayette. Instead, there are a series of "false summits" that present as one climbs; that is, you look ahead and up and think, "Oh there's the summit. That's not bad.", while in reality it is a ridge that once it is achieved just presents a hiker with another ridge that can also be confused for the summit and the process repeats. After a few repetitions it is only in the last mile that the true peak finally comes into view. By then the trail has leveled out and the walk up to the broad expanse of Lafayette's summit is exhilarating as one takes in the 360-degree views. Easily one of the best views in the northeast, Lafayette looks out across the vast expanse of the Pemigewasset Wilderness and takes in all the surrounding peaks: to the north and east the summits of Garfield, the Twins, the Bonds; to the east are Cannon, and the Kinsmans; and to the south are Lincoln, the spires of Liberty and Flume; and looking down one observes the wooded hump of Owls Head. It is easy to see why Lafayette is one of the more popular peaks in all the Whites. The effort of the climb pales in comparison with the rewards of the views on a good day.

It was time to move on to the next leg of the hike towards Liberty Springs. A little fuel added to the fire in the form of some trail mix and another bottle of water, and the two younger men were off and nearly out of site by the time Scott and Dave got moving. Dave spent much of the time on Lafayette lying flat and trying to stretch out the back muscles for some relief while Scott waited patiently. Packs slung back on and a look at the one mile stretch to Lincoln and they were off.

The trail descended off Lafayette at a welcome moderate grade as the two gradually became separated again due to Dave's significantly slower pace. There were a couple of minor ups and downs into the scrub brush but soon the trail steepened and climbed steadily to the summit of Lincoln. From this vantage point one can see the ribbon of trail strung out to the south along the knife edge of the ridge. No matter how many times one may see it, whether from the north or south, it is truly an awe-inspiring sight and when a hiker or two is seen traversing the ridge in the distance one gets a true understanding of the enormity and ruggedness of these mountains.

From Lincoln the trail descends steeply towards Little Haystack and follows the line of the knife edged ridge and gradually levels out making for fine walking on the well-maintained path. It was in this area the next issue cropped up for Dave: because of his slow pace and numerous stops to rest and ease the back spasms by this point he had drunk all the water he was carrying. There really wasn't too much longer to go to get to Liberty Springs to refill, but the brightness and breeze of the day coupled with the work being done across this ridge can sap a person of their bodily fluid levels and lead surprisingly quickly to the onset of dehydration. Not really too worried, he carried on and looked forward to dousing his thirst at Liberty Springs. However, as the afternoon went on, he found himself looking longingly at the muddy puddles he passed while trudging towards Little Haystack. Little did he know that less than a mile ahead of him Scott was having similar issues. He also was experiencing the pangs of dehydration and was plodding along in a bit of a fog with only one goal in mind: the spring. He got there and took out a small camp cup and guzzled it down about thirty times before laying down to rest.

Soon the summit of Little Haystack was achieved and after a quick steep descent the trail leveled out again and approached the junction of the Liberty Spring Trail. It was here that Dave, through his pain and thirst, saw Mike walking up the trail towards him. By now he and Marc had already been waiting at the tentsite for some time and when Scott finally arrived and was guzzling the sweet water of the spring to rehydrate Mike made the decision to fill his camelback and go back up the ridge to meet Dave in case he was having similar issues as Scott. He was a welcome sight to Dave and offered the nozzle of the camelback which was eagerly accepted and appreciated. Feeling refreshed the two walked on together slowly and descended from the ridge down the Liberty Spring Trail to the tentsite.

Mike and Marc had already secured a tent platform and the gear was dropped, the tents set up and a welcome rest was enjoyed. Scott continued to sip from Mikes camelback, Dave laid flat to ease his back pain, Marc was nursing his feet, and Mike mocked the old guys. Evening was coming on so soon it was time to make a little dinner of freeze-dried mac and cheese and enjoy the peace of the mountains. After a bit over a twelve-mile walk, sitting around the glow of the lamp as darkness fell was sweet reward. The fatigue was setting in and it wasn't long before the conversation waned, the other campsites fell quiet, and it was time for a well-earned rest before the hike down Liberty Springs Trail to the truck tomorrow.

Unfortunately, the morning dawned dark and overcast and it was certain to rain soon. Any thought of breakfast or morning coffee was dashed as the camp was quickly taken down, the packs loaded, and despite Mike and Marcs musing of going to grab Mts. Liberty and Flume, Dave offered that his only direction today was down the trail and the two relented and soon all four were dropping down the steep and rocky trail. Then the skies opened up and it poured! With just a relatively short way to go (about two miles +/-) no one bothered to stop and put on any rain gear, instead choosing to press on. The rocks became slick, and the trail became a stream in sections as the footfalls were carefully watched to avoid any falls. The trail moderated as it approached the junction of the Flume Slide Trail, and it wasn't long before the group could hear the hiss of the passing cars on Rt 93 in the distance. Fortunately, as the trailhead was neared it became evident that this was a passing heavy cloudburst and soon the rain began to let up and by the time they reached the parking area had nearly stopped.

Scott and Mike volunteered to take the truck back to the Garfield trailhead to get the car, and Dave and Marc gladly accepted their offer and took the time to rest in the wet grass and talk about this epic that had just completed. Marc was feeling proud of his achievement, and Dave was wishing to himself that he was Marcs age when he had begun this peakbagging effort. Soon the other two were back, the chairs were set up, the cooler pulled out and a proper celebration of the groups efforts commenced with the popping of four frosty cold Bud Lights and a toast was made to the mountains.

One of the best trips ever despite the "struggles". Right after arriving home Dave, having sworn to never allow dehydration to darken his travels, bought a 2+ liter camelback, and vowed to stretch better before tackling any trail in the future. *Each trip offers its own set of rewards and lessons, and if the mountains are speaking, it is best for any traveler to pay attention and learn.*

Despite the trials and tribulations of this trek across Franconia Ridge, after lengthy post hike discussions, both Dave and Scott agreed the experiences of the 2 days were a success. The mountain were speaking to them, and they heard the messages loud and clear. Injuries happen, preparation mistakes are made, and sometimes the weather just will not cooperate. Remain humble, over confidence is not a good hiking companion. Yet despite the obstacles, despite the unforeseen consequences, you must persevere, you must keep hiking. Dave's back injury put his physical and mental stamina to the ultimate test, and he passed with flying colors. No complaints, no quitting. Any hiker who has ever felt advancing dehydration, with the associated delirium, and the anxieties that prey on the mind knows all too well not to run out of water. Ever. Hiking in the pouring rain is never fun. Never. Both Dave and Scott became better hikers on this trip. Both felt a sincere, heartfelt satisfaction that they were able to hike with family, push themselves to new levels of exertion, while enjoying some of the best scenery in New England. Maybe the most important lesson learned is one that they already knew; *despite what personal struggles you may experience, each hiker has to keep an eye on each other*. Maybe that is the most important lesson of all and one they never forgot.

16. Cannon Mountain

"Getting to the top is optional. Getting down is mandatory."
Ed Viesturs

August 2007

Summer was easing by nicely and by mid-August life presented Dave and Scott with a mid-week opportunity to return to their happy place, the mountains. The focus for this trip would be back in Franconia Notch, specifically Cannon Mountain, a popular ski area standing at 4080 feet with views of a number of other 4000 footers in the White Mountain National Forest.

The usual early-ish start, cuppa coffee and a breakfast sandwich on the road as the day brightened to a clear summer day on the trip north and in short order, they found themselves at Lafayette Campground to secure a place for the night. Quick gear check for the climb, and a reconnaissance of the "post climb supplies": Chairs? Check. Beer? Check. OK.... Let's go!

The trail of choice today was going to be a quick two mile jaunt up the Kinsman Ridge trail to the summit and the two parked in the lot of the Cannon Mountain Tramway at the trailhead to begin their walk. The general idea today was to take their time to the ridge, enjoy the views over Franconia Notch to the east and to the Kinsman Range to the south and then maybe wander on over to the summit station of the tramway and grab a snack.

As had come to be expected any time when climbing out of the notch, the first few hundred yards of the trail were easy and simple…. and had also come to be expected, that didn't last long before the climbing began. Moving into the woods the trail began its ascent quickly and though there were a few switchbacks to make it a bit easier, the fact is that this stretch of the trail was pretty deeply eroded and very gravelly. It seemed through this section that each footfall was sliding back a bit as contact was being made with the loose soil, making for a more difficult climb as each step was calculated a little differently than the prior one.

Scott took the lead and the two eased their way through this area and soon broke out to some of the skiing trails. The good news was that they had moved out of the gravel walking mess. The bad news was that the trail remained quite steep and became rocky and ledgy and wetter. Having skied quite a bit when he was younger, Dave commented that even on his best days when younger he never would have attempted trails this steep, surmising that they had to be "Expert" trails for very skilled skiers. The trail crossed the slope a few times before reentering the woods and then began to moderate a bit, allowing Scott to pick up the pace. He was feeling pretty good and strong and when the trail permitted liked to "stretch it out" some and get the heart pumping even harder. Meanwhile, Dave was thinking, "The bastard" ………

However, Scotts' efforts proved to be worth it: after a short time the trail broke into a more open area and a side path lead down to a wide ledge that looked across the notch to the east and the vastness and beauty of the entire Franconia Range and down into the notch and the ribbon of I-93 below. This outlook was just above the sight of the Old Man of the

Mountain, the state symbol of New Hampshire that sadly collapsed in May of 2003. Stunning is not a strong enough word. The two lingered for a bit while having a few handfuls of trail mix, but there was still more work to be done and it became time to move on.

oking across to Franconia Ridge

The trail began its moderate climb briefly before dropping down into a wet area just to add a little bit of an extra pain in the butt before climbing steeply once again and reaches the Rim Trail; for lack of a better term, it is the "tourist trail" used by folks who take the Tramway up the mountain to the summit. A nice easy walk to the crowded summit tower and another peak was in the bag.

The view from the tower was, as expected, magnificent. 360 degrees of pure beauty stretched out. However, looking to the west towards Vermont some ominous clouds were building. Having taken their time getting to the trailhead and up the mountain it was now early afternoon and it appeared that a summer storm was brewing. Dave turned to Scott and suggested it may be about time to beat a retreat to the trail and soon enough they were headed back to the shelter of the woods.

It wasn't long before the rumble of distant thunder began to echo through the mountains, and it was pretty obvious this was going to be a doozy of a storm. As they turned off the rim trail and back down into the sag the sky was quickly darkening, and flashes of lightning were becoming evident. A sense of urgency replaced the usual calm after a successful summit. The pace quickened to a trot as they recrossed the ledgy area and by the time they reached the ski slope the storm was nearly on top of them. Interestingly there was no rain yet, just the flashbangs of lightning and near instant thunder crashing overhead. Back down to the steep gravel section and no words were being spoken in the effort of pure concentration to watch each step and get down and to the safety of the truck as fast as possible.

Though it was only midafternoon the sky took on the hue of twilight as the storm raged closer and as the two hikers broke out into the clearing and the last few hundred yards to the truck they broke into a sprint as what seemed to be near constant thunder exploded all around.

There would be no sitting out and basking in the success of this hike today as finally the clouds opened up and the deluge started. A couple of beers were grabbed from the cooler and as the boys jumped into the truck another instant flashbang essentially said to the hikers, "GET OUT AND STAY OUT!!!!" as though the mountain Gods had had enough of them this day.

While waiting for the storm to wane the two discussed the fact that despite all the preparation they usually took for each trip, the one wild card will always be the weather. The forecast for the day did indeed say possible thunderstorms, but in all reality, is a trip going to be cancelled based on a possibility? *One must remember always that not everything is within your control.* They were wise enough to keep an eye on the sky this day and despite the fact they were chased off the mountain they at least had the wisdom to get out before things got too bad. They were fortunate to be safe and vowed that weather watching was also going to become part of the pre-trip repertoire.

When they returned to the campground, as expected it was a soggy mess and neither really felt like breaking out the grill to make any dinner, so Scott made the Executive Decision that tonight dinner would be down the road at the Woodstock Inn and Brewery. The rain had stopped, so time was made to set up the tent and prepare (and cover) the wood for the fire upon the return. The food was excellent, the brews were cold and the camaraderie solid as dinner was enjoyed and followed by a nice fire on a comfortable June night.

Although the hike was rewarding as usual, and the views terrific, their thoughts by the fire turned to the storm, and the dangers of getting caught in intense storms while hiking. The mountain spoke loudly to them that day and the lesson was neither subtle nor understated. *When it's time to take cover, and time to leave one must not hesitate.* This became a lesson that would have to be heard once and once only.

Notable: On September 10, 2022, a good friend and hiking companion Don ventured to Franconia Notch and Cannon Mountain to complete his 48th and final peak on a beautiful early autumn day. Don, a former Army Black Hawk helicopter pilot, joined Scott and Dave for the trip to their final peak in 2012. That trip was his first summit, actually his first 3, as he bagged Mt. Washington, Mt. Monroe, and Mt. Isolation on that same epic trip. Obviously, he caught the hiking bug as well; ten years later he cruised up Cannon and proudly posed for the commemoration of his tremendous efforts. Like Rodney (who completed all 48 with him), Don became an excellent hiker, who complained little and always brought excellent conversation and companionship to any hiking party. He was known for always carrying red Twizzlers on all his trips. Dave and Scott had spent many evenings around a campfire with both Don and Rodney, and were proud that both had accomplished this amazing goal. Another example of friendships forged hiking in the White Mountains.

Rodney, Don, and Scott celebrate Don's 48th!

17. Carter Dome and Wildcat Mountain

"When preparing to climb a mountain – pack a light heart."
Dan May

October 2007

Although they never thought long and hard about winter hiking, both guys were interested in maybe "pushing the envelope" a bit and attempting some later fall hiking. After a bit of research, they decided to tackle Carter Dome, the ninth highest peak, and Wildcat A; with the plan being to include an overnight stay at the Carter Notch hut. The hut full-service season was over, but it was open on a self-service basis. Hikers could pay a nominal fee and utilize the kitchen for meal preparation and sleep in the bunk house. This sounded exactly like what they were looking for, the decision was made, and off they drove to the Mt. Washington area for the 2-day adventure.

Getting an early start, after stopping for a coffee at Dunkin Donuts, they arrived at the trailhead of the Nineteen Mile Brook Trail relatively early in the morning. The packs were loaded with 2 days' worth of food, sleeping bags, warm clothes and plenty of water and snacks. It was a very nice late October day, with good temperatures for hiking. The foliage was mostly gone, and except for a few late trees, darker browns, and faded golds dominated the mountainsides.

Beginning the day, they set off on the scenic Nineteen Mike Brook Trail, which is considered to be the easiest route to the Carter Notch Hut. The trail meandered along the beautiful Nineteen Mile Brook, the constant sound of rushing water in the background made for a more relaxing start to what promised to be a busy day. The trail begins relatively flat, passing an old dam, as well as a small cascade before it reaches the junction of the Carter Dome trail at 1.9 miles. Scott remarked how this trail was not only scenic but was a very enjoyable way to start the day. The walk would become much steeper, culminating at the height of land and the junction of the Wildcat Ridge Trail at 3.6 miles. From here the trail drops steeply toward the Carter Notch Hut, passing the beautiful Carter Lake. The mountain lakes never disappoint, as they are Mother Nature at her finest. Pristine scenery, sparking clean water, nestled in the Cater Moriah Range. To this point in the morning, both hikers were enjoying the hike, taking in the scenery, and feeling pretty strong. It was around this time in the quest to conquer all 48 peaks, that both were hitting their stride with their hiking ability; although each hiking adventure began with a few "butterflies" because of never knowing fully what to expect, each man had become both physically and mentally prepared for each adventure. That, combined with the valuable experiences gained with each trip, translated into two very positive and confident hikers, thoroughly enjoying each different adventure. That is not to say that each hiking adventure didn't include some pain and discomfort along the way. That goes without saying.

Arriving at the Carter Notch Hut around noontime they checked in to the hut and scanned the facility, neither having visited there prior. and found the kitchen and bunk house, where they would sleep tonight. Having walked approximately 3.8 miles, they ate lunch at the hut, and discussed the afternoon plans, a 1.2 mile climb to the summit of Carter Dome with about 1500 feet of elevation gain, no small task.

Well rested and fed, Dave and Scott began the afternoon's hike with lightened packs and set out on the Carter Moriah Trail to the summit. This trail extends 13.8 miles north of Mt. Washington and the Presidential Range. It includes six formidable mountains, however only four count toward the goal of summitting all 48 peaks. The trail started off relatively steeply passing a beautiful view of Carter Notch, including a marvelous overlook of a jumble of boulders called the Ramparts. It then moderates a bit before it reaches the open summit. Beautiful views of Pinkham Notch, as well as many of the Presidentials highlighted what was a great day of hiking in the White Mountains in late October. The two stayed on the summit for maybe a half hour or so, before heading back down to the hut. The days were certainly getting much shorter this time of year, and neither wanted to attempt a descent in less than optimum conditions.

The Ramparts

An uneventful descent put them back at the hut around 4:30 pm or so, hungry and a bit tired. Both were looking forward to the nice pasta dinner Scott would prepare in the kitchen. They had the place all to themselves. As expected, the dinner was delicious, filling the growling bellies, and putting them one step closer to a well-deserved and quiet, albeit chilly nights sleep in the mountains. As expected, sleep came early.

The next morning would prove to be one of the more embarrassing moments in the entire odyssey of these guy's adventures in the White Mountains. Although planning to get an early start in the morning as they still had to climb Wildcat A to finish the planned itinerary, they did not get that early start. For some reason, unexplainable to either, both slept until almost 10 AM! Maybe it was the solitude of the mountains, maybe it was having the hut to themselves or maybe they were just tired. Neither guy was a late sleeper, especially when there was much work to do. So many times, they had always awakened on time, ready for the next days adventure, but not on this particular day. *Don't let the small setbacks ruin a day. Address them, regroup, and carry on.*

Not willing to delay the pending day's work any longer, Dave made some breakfast in the kitchen, they packed the bags and set forth up the Wildcat Ridge Trail. Ahead was approximately .7 of a mile, with about 1000 feet of elevation gain to accomplish the goals for this trip. The weather was extremely overcast, with light rain falling making the ascent more miserable than had been hoped. Still reeling from the late start, in addition to hiking in less than optimal conditions, they summitted Wildcat A in relatively short order. It may have been their shortest stay on any mountain to date. No view, just a light rain. A less than memorable descent left 3.6 miles along the Nineteen Mike Brook Trail back to the vehicle in the early afternoon.

The weather did improve a bit as the men reached the vehicle, thus enabling them to take out the chairs, slide off the boots and have a couple ice cold beers. As always, they discussed the trip at length, highlights, and lowlights. Both determined that this trip was a huge success; they had never hiked this late in the year, had never been to this particular hut after the close of the season, and had taken in some beautiful views in the process. Preparation and execution of the trip went smoothly, even though they "overslept". Improvements needed for sure, but each new experience made them better, more confident, and more adaptable hikers for sure.

This hike would mark the end of the hiking season for them, satisfied with a very successful year in which they summitted six more 4000 foot peaks and leaving them looking ahead for the next great adventure.

Unlike the loud, clear and thunderous lesson Dave and Scott heard on Mt Cannon, the mountains voice was much more quiet and definitely more subtle on this trip. They actually had to listen. The message of these two October days in the Carter Moriah Range were not of lack of preparation, or troublesome weather, or even physical exhaustion. Rather it was of Solitude. *Mother Nature is best served with peace and quiet; the mountains told them to not be in a rush. Enjoy your time in the mountains, free from the clamor of normal everyday life. Make Solitude your strength.*

18. South Carter

"Nature does not hurry, yet everything is accomplished"
Lao Tzu

Early Summer 2008

The winter of '07-'08 had worn on far too long and Scott and Dave kept themselves busy by hiking many of the local trails in their area of northeastern CT to keep in shape. Spring finally rolled around, and the plans were afoot to continue the peakbagging quest. The focus was once again on the Pinkham Notch area and the Carter-Moriah Range, specifically South Carter. Both men had busy work schedules, so it was decided to turn a quick overnighter and knock that one off the list.

An early morning start got them to Dolly Copp Campground before 9:00 AM to pick the ideal camping spot near the river and by 10:00 they were once again at the Nineteen Mile Brook trailhead to begin the day. Having walked Nineteen Mile Brook Trail when they completed Carter Dome the season before, the men knew this would be a pleasant walk on this clear, very windy morning. There were only a couple of other cars at the parking area, so it promised to be a day mostly alone on the trail, which suited them just fine.

The first couple of miles went easily as expected and they took in the sights of this beautiful trail once again as the conversation flowed and the wind howled in the new leaves of the forest. It wasn't even an hour in, and they came to the junction of the Carter Dome Trail and turned left and began to climb steadily, but there were several switchbacks making the climb significantly easier towards Zeta Pass, the first goal of the day.

Having kept in good shape over the winter made the miles melt away and it was a bit over an hour later the junction with the Carter-Moriah Trail was achieved at Zeta Pass and it was time for a short break. Having both been taught a lesson from last year's Garfield and Franconia traverse and the agony of dehydration both men decided that there would be no more carrying of a couple of bottles of water on their hikes: each had purchased at least 2-liter Camelbaks to put to bed any more risk of running into that issue ever again. Additionally, Dave had bought a Lifestraw in case of the unlikely possibility they would run out of water again. At least they could drink from a stream or small pond if required. This time there would be no camping at a shelter, so the heavy packs were jettisoned for much more compact daypacks.

Relaxing for a snack on the large rocks beside the trail, a lone hiker approached the from the south. He had just come off nearby Mount Hight and it was easy to see he was exhilarated and feeling chatty. He had camped near the summit the prior night and was awaked by the winds early that morning. He was loving the windstorm and mentioned that a couple of times he was nearly blown off his feet on the summit and spent hours just watching and listening to the roar before he decamped and started heading back towards Pinkham. Scott offered that maybe they should go up Hight to experience it, but the goal was still set on the 4000 Footers and sadly Mt. Hight was another one of those peaks not on the list. It is considered a shoulder of Carter Dome, even though it is over 4600 feet tall.. The choice was made to push ahead, and complete South Carter and they turned north on the Carter-Moriah Trail.

It was a nice easy walk with little effort required as the trail descended a bit first, levelled off for a bit more before making a quick ascent to the wooded summit of South Carter, just a few yards off the main trail. Frankly, it was a bit of an anticlimax in both hikers' minds after the way they felt going up. There is no view from the summit, which was expected but the adrenaline was pumping, and it was a bit of a letdown. Nonetheless, it was another peak in the bag: Number 29!! Time to work the way back down the trail to the rewards of the day.

In retrospect, however, this was another one of those opportunities to bag another peak that was allowed to slide by. That is, Middle Carter was only another 1.3 miles up the trail. They had done this several times; be essentially within shouting distance of another 4000 Footer and they chose not to do it. This time it wasn't fatigue, it wasn't the steepness of the trail as it was a fairly level and easy hike along this section of the Appalachian Trail. No, this time it appeared another storm was brewing, and they chose wisely. *When an opportunity is passed up, but the chance will be there again one day, don't be too heavy on yourself.*

However, they turned back south and were soon again at Zeta Pass and heading down the Carter Dome Trail. They hit Nineteen Mile Brook and then turned up the speed and were back at the parking area in less than an hour.

As with all of their hikes, pre hike preparation was essential including plans for the day. Dave and Scott embarked on this day with the thought that if the conditions were right, including their physical and mental stamina, they would also try to summit Middle Carter as well. Grabbing Middle Carter would add 2.6 miles to an almost 10-mile trip. However, when they arrived on South Carter, they noticed an ominous storm cloud enveloping Middle Carter. The entire summit and surrounding area were blanketed in a shroud of darkness; after a very brief discussion, both came to the agreement that this peak should be attempted on another day. They turned back toward Zeta pass, enduring some incredible winds, now looking back across the Carter Moriah Trail, both comfortable with the decision. As was customarily the case, Dave set off down the Carter Dome trail in a blistering pace, setting the tone for an extremely rapid descent. Soon they found themselves once again on the Nineteen Mile Brook Trail, extolling its ease and its beauty.

Soon they found themselves back at their vehicle but this time it was decided that they would take their post hike celebration to a different place; they would set up across from the Mt. Washington auto road, away from traffic and enjoy a few beers while glancing at the Presidentials, notably Mt Washington. Dave prepared some of the best tasting hot dogs, with all the fixings and the two recapped their day enjoying the scenery, having just completed almost 10 miles and the 29th 4000 footer to date. The day was a success despite not summitting Middle Carter.

The days lesson was a repeat of other trips, notably Mt Cannon. *No unnecessary risks in the mountains; if the weather turns for the worse, safety is paramount.* It was a lesson that both Dave and Scott agreed and always followed without fail.

There would be an overnight at Dolly Copp campground by the fire and plans were being made for the next adventure. A great way to end an ideal day in the mountains.

19. Wildcat D

"If you find a path with no obstacles, it probably doesn't lead anywhere."
Frank A. Clark

Summer 2008

Summer was wearing on, and at a get-together with family and several friends, Scott floated the idea that it was about time for a group trip. Up to this point, he and Dave had walked with others on a few occasions, but the thought was to see if there were any others in their circle who may consider summitting a 4000 Footer. Almost immediately there were four takers who jumped on board enthusiastically! Plans were made for a two night trip to really allow the "newcomers" to get a feel for fun and adventure of hiking a 4000 foot peak and then later enjoying the feeling of (hopefully) success and camaraderie of sitting around a campfire after. This time Scott and Dave would be joined by Scott's bother Bob, Bob's son Brian, their old friend Rusty, and a co-worker friend of Dave's named Jack. Vehicle arrangements were made, menus laid out and decisions of who would bring what were made and within a week, the group was off and heading back to Dolly Copp to hit the Wildcat Ridge Trail and grab Wildcat D.

This peak was chosen because: Scott and Dave needed to check it off their list; It was a relatively short hike out of the ski area parking lot (only a 4.2 mile out and back); it offered the rewards of a great view (weather permitting), as well as a bail out (the ski lift running for the sightseers) if anyone felt they needed it after the ascent. The crew loaded up three vehicles with their gear and food and were off on a Thursday afternoon with a planned rally point in Lincoln for a bite to eat and then off to Dolly Copp Campground in the Pinkham Notch area to set up for the night. It wasn't long before the fire was built, the tents set up, the cooking gear prepared and the music playing as this gang settled in for a sweet evening of banter, ball-busting, and some beer drinking. However, knowing there was work to do the next day, they kept things in check, and all were bedded down early for a fresh start in the morning.

The day dawned clear and fresh, and a hearty camp breakfast was assembled to fuel the group for the trip ahead. Scott had made a pot of coffee for any takers, and this proved to be some real high-octane java to get the blood flowing. Hopping into the cars the plan was to meet down Rt 16 at the Glen Ellis Falls parking area, go through the underpass, and hit the Wildcat Ridge Trail, which is also part of the Appalachian Trail.

As Scott and Dave had discovered, many of the trails leading out of the three major notches typically start getting steep quickly…really quickly, and this trail was no exception. An easy crossing of the Ellis River was followed quickly by climbing up the end of the Wildcat Ridge leading to a rocky cliff side ascent up a series of rough rock steps that caused the group to separate somewhat. Brian, being the youngest member of the group surged ahead easily, with Scott, Rusty and Jack coming along not too far behind. Rusty had done a couple of the 4000 footers before, most notably the Zealand and Bond trip a few years ago with Scott and Dave, and as was his usual rarely stopped and always maintained a steady methodical pace. Dave attributed his ability to do that to Rusty's military experience. The man knew how to march. Not too far behind Dave was walking with Bob and sharing some of his climbing experiences and doing his best to keep Bob's mind off the growing pain in his legs. Things were going to be rough for a while and he didn't want Bob to get discouraged, however he knew Bob well enough to understand the man had no quit in him.

They completed this cliff side section, and the trail moderated a bit and the guys in front paused to let the rest of the group catch up in a small clearing with a view across Pinkham Notch towards Washington. A quick handful of trail mix, a sip from the Camelbak and they were off again to face the next, even more daunting, obstacle. About a mile and half in the trail comes to what could best be described as a chimney presenting a really steep and narrow ascent up the side of another cliff. As the group approached there was a couple coming down after climbing about half-way up this obstacle due to the fact that the less experienced girlfriend had decided she would not attempt it. A couple of the members of the group looked at each other as if to ask if they should attempt it, but after some encouragement they plunged right into it. Russ took the lead and picked his way up the face, followed by Brian and Jack with Bob, Scott and Dave bringing up the rear. It had its moments of giving pause as they scrambled up but soon the entire group was on top as the trail levelled off. The views to the west were spectacular as they paused to look across the notch into the ravines of Mount Washington. This is what Scott and Dave were hoping for the rest of the crew: to reap the rewards of glorious scenery stretched out before them and to cement in their minds that *the pain is worth it*.

Mt. Washington from Wildcat

From there it was a relatively easy jaunt through some leftover snow in the shaded areas as they passed by Wildcats East Peak and soon found themselves near the summit at the terminus of the ski area. A short, but steep climb up to the summit and to the tower gave everyone a well earned feeling of satisfaction. Scott expressed a little disappointment at the number of "tourists" who were sharing the top. To him, getting to the summit in a gondola just didn't quite seem fair after all the effort that is required to climb up. But, to each their own and at least these folks were out enjoying the mountain scenery and fresh air.

While the crew sat on some open slabs sunning themselves the questions began to arise as to whether they all wanted to descend certain sections of the trail, particularly the steep ridges and slabs as well as the chimney. Taking the lift down was absolutely out of the question, however being that the ski slopes were mostly clear it became an option to descend by walking down one of the slopes to the parking area at the base. After some discussion they decided to descend via the Polecat Trail to the base of the mountain.

The slope was not an "expert" or "Double Black Diamond", as it wound its way around the side of the ski area. The views were great but being that it was still fairly early in the summer there were some very muddy sections that were difficult to circumvent. But the trip down was uneventful and soon they arrived at the parking area. Rusty somehow snagged a ride to the parking area where the vehicles were parked and returned shortly to pick up the gang and in no time they were once again firmly ensconced at Dolly Copp and enjoying the rewards of their efforts as Russ put out a huge pasta dinner.

The laughter around the fire that night over the failures and victories of the day seemed to echo through the mountains as the aches and pains started to set in. But….no one was complaining…… it was a great day with a great group.

Rusty, Dave, Scott, and Jack

20. Mount Moosilauke

"Of all the paths you take in life, make sure a few of them are dirt."
John Muir

September 2008

Fall was approaching and it had been busy summers for both Dave and Scott and unfortunately that prevented them from getting back to the mountains as often as they would have preferred. Not to let the hiking season slip away without one more peak and after a bit of discussion regarding how much time could be cobbled together, they decided on a trip to the Lincoln/Woodstock area to climb Mt. Moosilauke. They opted for a mid-September weekday trip attempting to avoid the hordes of tourists and leaf peepers that descend on this area, mostly on the weekend.

Part of the learning process in selecting which peak to tackle, the guys were paying close attention to the weather conditions for each and every trip. Some lessons were learned the hard way, having a few trips aborted all together. Six plus hours of driving is not recommended in vain, as both

Dave and Scott were at a busy point in their lives. In addition, a careful check of the weather ensures a much more enjoyable night camping under the stars. Anyone who spends any amount of time in the White Mountains knows full well that the weather is unpredictable and subject to change on a moments notice. Always a potential danger while climbing.

With that said, the trip to Mt Moosilauke took a unique turn; a hurricane was scheduled to batter New England on the intended day of travel. Maybe it was an evolving sense of adventure, or maybe the two felt that they needed to get this last peak in 2008, therefore, they made the decision to go forward with the trip, despite the weather predictions. Careful review of the forecast did indicate that the storm would be passed on the day of the climb. Also, further review of the potential path of the storm revealed that the full brunt of the cyclone would "most likely" miss the northern interior New Hampshire. Additional discussions were not necessary, the trip was a go. If anything changed, a hotel room would be a safe option.

The weather was indeed a bit ominous as Dave and Scott were driving to Russell Pond Campground near Woodstock, NH. They had stayed at this campground previously; it did have shelters, warm showers, and was close to town if the weather deteriorated. As the morning drew on, it was evident that the hurricane had taken the more predictable path offshore and the rain and wind had subsided a bit, enough to allow them to set up camp. They arrived at Russell Pond, a beautiful campground nestled in the Sandwich Range, located near a very scenic pond, which during nicer weather is utilized for fishing, kayaking, and swimming. A return to this campground again was in the cards for sure. Tents were set up, and soon they found themselves enjoying a cold beer by a crackling fire, wondering why they fretted at all about the weather. They enjoyed a hearty meal of "chuckwagon stew", prepared by Scott's wife, an excellent pre hike meal.

However, the rain returned as expected with a vengeance and an enjoyable night by the fire ended abruptly as the two retreated to their respective tents, hunkered down from the pelting rain. The men stayed relatively dry throughout the night despite the rivers of rainwater cascading through the camp site. Next morning dawned mostly overcast as they packed the drenched camping gear, put on some dry hiking clothes, got their packs ready and drove off to breakfast in Woodstock.

Moosilauke offers several different trails to the summit of varying difficulty and distance and the choice was to begin at the Moosilauke Ravine Lodge, owned by the Dartmouth College Outing Club. It is at the end of a dirt road off Route 118, not too far from Route 93. Access was fairly easy, allowing them to park near the lodge and in short order they were on a brief descent, crossing a foot bridge, then onto the Gorge Brook Trail. Because of this mountains' proximity to the lodge, there are numerous trails to the summit, therefore close attention must be paid to remain on the intended trails. The Asquam Ridge Trail veers off to the right, the Hurricane Trail (aptly named for this trip) went left and the preferred Gorge Brook Trail goes straight ahead. Fortunately, as (almost) always, proper signage removes any doubt in a hikers mind.

Soon they found themselves back into the wilderness, beginning a moderately steep climb up the 10th tallest mountain in northern New Hampshire. Moosilauke is 4802 feet tall, and this ascent would require about 2450 feet of elevation gain in about 3.9 miles. The trail changes from easy to relatively more moderate grades, but never becomes uncomfortably steep. It passes a few clear outlooks, however on this overcast day, no views were to be seen. After a few steeper switchbacks at 3.5 miles, the trail reaches a shoulder and opens up and offers a great view of the rounded open summit. Both were feeling strong and comfortable with the pace up to the actual top; as they approached the sign indicating the actual summit, they both remarked on what a well maintained trail they had just traveled. Dave commented and expressed appreciation for the hardy and rugged crews who maintain these trails so all can enjoy them safely.

As had been the case throughout the ascent this day remained cloudy and overcast offering very little views off the fantastic, open rounded peak. This mountain would have to be attempted again; they could only imagine the 360 degree view on a clear day. In fact, both Dave and Scott had earlier expressed interest in making this mountain their 48th, based on all they had heard and read about the views on this summit. There is an orange sign on the top denoting the actual highest point. As they sat at the base of the sign enjoying some lunch the amazing thing to both men was that there wasn't another human to be seen. Granted, it wasn't the best day weather-wise, and it was mid-week but on such a lovely mountain it seemed odd to be alone. Neither complained one bit.

As the two hikers pondered the descent, anticipating rain at any time, they were approached by two other hikers emerging through the fog from the south. They were both excited, and their pace quickened up the last section, and finally reached the summit in short order. One of the hikers turned to Scott and Dave and shouted that this was his 48th peak. He was done! Congratulations and handshakes were given and the four shared some of their adventures of their quests.

Approaching the summit

Both Dave and Scott were not only impressed with his accomplishments, but this meeting hardened their resolve to finish what they had started a few years ago. Buoyed by this turn of events, they raced down the mountain, and in no time found themselves back at the lodge. Feeling a little sore, but much more confident and determined to finish their goal of "bagging the 48", celebratory beers were in order. It would have been easy to not make this trip due to weather concerns; however, the coincidence of being on the same summit as two other hikers, on the day after a hurricane, with one of them completing his 48th peak, is very hard to explain. Just another one of those great and sometimes unexpected hiking experiences. Dave and Scott could see the light at the end of the tunnel as Mt Moosilauke was their 32nd peak, 16 to go. No problem.

Back at the campsite, as they sat around the fire that evening, the storm long gone, they reflected on the events of the past couple days. A hurricane did not deter them, and they bagged the tenth highest mountain in New Hampshire. They were learning, again and again that with each trip, each adventure, one gains strength, courage, and confidence. *Sometimes it is better to venture out of your comfort zone, seeking new adventures that can lead to even more rewarding and gratifying experiences,* even on a cloudy, rainy, and windy day in the mountains. Lesson learned.

What's next in 2009?

An additional note: Our hikers revisited Mt. Moosilauke again on September 9, 2016. Their close friend and hiking mate, Rodney, had contracted the 4000 foot bug from Scott and Dave in 2011 when he bagged Owls Head while accompanying the old guys. After that first, long trek in the Pemigewasset Wilderness, the fever in him grew quickly and soon he was well into the quest, hiking with his wife, his son, and other friends. Rodney made it a point to join the team when Scott and Dave completed their 48th atop Mt. Isolation, and consequently, as they were there for Rodney's 1st peak, it was an honor and an obligation to be there for his 48th. Appropriately, Rodney chose to hike his final peak on the day every year in Sept that Flags on the 48 is held. It was another cloudy start to the journey, but fittingly the skies cleared as the group approached the summit for the culmination of Rodney's quest. The pride was evident as Rodney, Dave and Scott posed for a photo at the summit sign with the US flag flying above them as congratulations were extended to him by the crowd at the summit for the commemoration.

Rodney's 48th!!

21. Mount Moriah

"Choose only one master-Nature"
Rembrandt

Memorial Day Weekend 2009

Next on the list for Dave and Scott was to attack another section of the beautiful Carter Moriah Trail and the northernmost 4000 footer in that range: Mount Moriah, a relatively small (4049 ft) peak northeast of Mount Washington. The actual summit is on the Appalachian Trail and the plan was to hike the Stony Brook Trail for 3.6 miles then join the difficult Carter Moriah Trail for approximately a mile and a half for the trek to the summit. The day's work would consist of a ten mile out and back and encompass approximately 3100 feet of elevation gain to complete.

In keeping with their recent tradition, the trip took place on Memorial Day, when most of the snow is gone from the lower elevations and it to them, was the unofficial kickoff to the summer hiking season. Dave and Scott had been asking friends and family members to join them for this long three-day weekend and were pleased to be joined once again by

Scotts' brother Bob, son Mike, nephew Marc, and old friend Russ as the rendezvoused at Dolly Copp Campground for a weekend of camping, camaraderie, and climbing. This trip would also include Scotts family dog Riley, a beautiful yellow lab who was on her maiden hiking trip.

After a comfortable night camping, the group collaborated on a solid breakfast and were at the Stony Brook Trailhead not far from Gorham right around 8:00 AM, geared up and ready to go. The early morning weather was a bit overcast at first, but all the weather reports (particularly the Mount Washington Observatory high peaks forecast) indicated that it would clear and remain cool throughout the day. Good hiking conditions for sure. The Stony Brook Trail begins by crossing a footbridge over the brook and nearly parallels it for about a mile of relatively flat walking, a good start to get the muscles warmed up and moving. Moods were high and the conversation flowed easily for the group with topics including old high school football exploits, past girlfriends, and the Boston Red Sox. Soon enough Mike and Marc took off on their usual fast pace with Riley and were not to be seen again until the summit. The trail began ascending moderately and after about 2.3 miles crosses the brook once again and gets steep for the push up to the Carter Moriah Trail. This section of the hike proved to be the most strenuous of the day with no scenery to absorb and inspire but would be rewarded when they joined the Carter Moriah Trail in about another half-mile.

This portion of the Carter Moriah Trail for the 1.4 miles to the summit was a nice, moderate ascent along open ridges and slabs and afforded numerous viewpoints north and east into Maine, Evans Notch, and west to Pinkham Notch and the Presidentials. Any scenic section of a hike, near the treelines or along open ledges is a welcome sight for any hiker and this section did not disappoint. The trail continued along the south ridge of Moriah and opens to a massive clearing, which at first glance could be confused for the summit. A quick turn to the north however revealed the beautiful peak, still partially covered in snow. The group made their way through the remaining snow in the shaded areas and came to a short but steep scramble to the actual summit where the flat, open crest provided beautiful views in all directions making the five mile effort even more rewarding. The gang soaked in the views while having a snack before scrambling off the top and beginning their descent with yet another renewed sense of pride and accomplishment that would spur them on to what hopefully would be a successful hiking season ahead.

Atop Moriah

Michael and Marc (and Riley) had larger plans for the day ahead as they would continue on the Carter Moriah Trail past the Stony Brook intersection and would continue across North Carter Mountain. From there they had Middle Carter in their sights to summit, and then a trip down the

Imp Trail back to Rt 16. This would extend their day almost another 8 miles and they would bag another 4000 footer. A great days' effort.

As the older members of the group continued across the open slabs of Moriah, the pace was brisk, and all felt really good. However, as Dave was walking along an open ledge, he was too busy laughing at one of Bobs jokes and wasn't paying attention to his footfalls. One small broken branch was all it took for him to step on as it rolled under his boot, and he went down onto the rock with a thud. He had tried to use his trekking pole to stabilize and in so doing he somehow wedged the pole between himself and the slab and despite the pole being planted he fell right across on the way down. The good news is he didn't hit his head; the not so good news was that he bent his trekking pole nearly in half as he fell right across it using his ribs to break the fall! A moment of concern from the group and a few mutters of "I'm all right" and soon the group was moving again, although Dave, feeling like he likely cracked a rib was moving much more slowly. *Not only are they inspiring, but never forget mountains also teach one modesty.*

However, it wasn't long before they hit the Stony Brook junction and back into the viewless woods for the descent. Conversation once again flowed and in what seemed like no time at all the group arrived back at the trailhead. The feeling of arriving back at one's vehicle after a successful hiking adventure in the White Mountains is like no other. Take the boots off, crack a cold one and debrief the days events, particularly having a good chuckle at Dave's clumsiness.

After picking up Mike and Marc further down Rt 16 the group was soon back at Dolly Copp for a sweet night of food, fire and friends as the next trip was already being planned. Next up tomorrow? Plans for Mount Waumbek were already in progress.

Dave and Scott were sincerely enjoying the camaraderie on these hiking trips, having spent a great deal of time on the trails by themselves over the past 10 years. Planning these Memorial Day trips was fun, as well as mapping out each trip taking into consideration individual hiking ability, interest, and stamina. *Hike as much, or as little as you want, no one will question your decisions. When hiking, judgment should always take the front seat.*

22. Mount Waumbek

"Mountains should not be judged by altitude."
Louis L'Amour

Memorial Day Weekend 2009

A good and comfortable night around the fire after the successful ascent of Mt Moriah and the gang was up early the next morning, and though the older members were feeling a bit stiff and sore, the younger crew was ready to tackle the next goal today: 4006 ft. Mt Waumbek. Although it is 7.2 miles out and back, the thinking was that because it is a relatively smaller 4000 footer and didn't offer too much in the way of steepness and difficulty that it would make for a good second day climb.

Rather than take multiple vehicles the crew all loaded into Russ's RV for the ride to the trailhead and were on the road shortly after 8:00 AM fueled up with a good breakfast and a heaping helping of caffeine. The Memorial Day weekend weather looked great with clear skies and a warm breeze from the south. At the trailhead it didn't take long to gear up, check the packs for the necessities, and make sure there was plenty of water.

Although still early in the season, a few members opted for simple tee shirts and shorts for this trip and Scott couldn't help but notice that Marc was wearing cut-off jeans as his attire. Now, none of this group deserved any awards for their mountain fashion sense by any means, however the choice of jean shorts drew some significant ribbing upon Marc, and he quickly was dubbed "Jortsy" .... and soon after the moniker was completed with the last name of Waumbek as he became the "Official Mascot" of the day. *Amongst the best things about hiking with friends is not only the feeling of a combined sense of purpose, but also the fact that a day of ribbing and teasing makes the miles fun.*

Jortsy Waumbek and Mike took off quickly as the group hit the Starr King Trail, a well maintained and marked path under the purview of the Randolph Mountain Club. The elder members came along behind as they worked the kinks and aches out of their limbs on the old logging road that is the beginning of the trail. As people fell into their rhythm the group spread out a bit with the younger men (and Riley) soon out of sight and the others walking in single file and enjoying the morning air. Leaving the logging road, the trail began a nice ascent up the ridge of Mt. Starr King with excellent footing before cutting off to the left and traversing the side of the slope until it began a quick ascent up to the summit for about only a tenth of a mile. Once upon a time there was a shelter at the top of Starr King, and all that remains is a large stone fireplace as a place to rest and reconnoiter and snap a photo or two before the trail enters the woods again and commences to become a nice ridge walk between Starr King and the summit of Waumbek. The mile between the peaks went quickly and soon the entire crew was reunited on the mostly wooded summit that is marked with a cairn. High fives were shared as yet another 4000 footer was in the books. This weekends' work brought Scott and Dave up to a total of 34 completed thus far.

The trip down was easy and breezy as everyone was feeling good and strong and they found themselves back at the RV quickly, having turned the 7.2 mile out and back trip in a little over five hours. Little time was wasted packing up and hitting the road again as everyone had one destination in mind: Mr. Pizza in Gorham was one of Mikes favorite eateries when in the mountains and there would be no denying him of that pleasure. An hour or so of devouring greasy appetizers and multiple large pizzas and the hunger was quelled as it became time to head back to Dolly Copp for a very chilly swim in the Peabody River and to relax the remainder of the day away sharing stories and laughs.

A great start to the 2009 season and Dave and Scott, though feeling the satisfaction and the burn of the weekends' efforts, were already looking ahead to the next peak to try to conquer as they hoped to put a good dent in the list of remaining 4000 foot peaks.

Positivity was at the forefront of the guys' mindset as they entered the final phase of their mission. The end was in sight, and both were feeling confident heading into 2009. The sum total of experiences over the past 10 or so years, both negative and positive, provided them with a template for completion of their goal. *Stay positive, stay healthy and humble.* Both were appreciative of the lessons the mountains had taught them and looking forward to finishing their goal of summitting all the 48 four thousand footers in the White Mountains.

23. Mount Jefferson Solo

"Failure is the condiment that gives success its flavor."
Truman Capote

June 2009

Still reeling from the embarrassment from not completing Mt Jefferson the first time in 2003, Scott saw an opportunity to not only rid himself of the demons of the past failure, but to accomplish something he had been wanting to do for some time; hike solo. No time to revel in the past, it was 2009 and Scott (and Dave) were different hikers at this point in the process. They were stronger physical hikers, better prepared and better equipped for sure. In addition, and probably most importantly, the two hiking partners were much tougher mentally, looking forward to each hike with positive anticipation and a much more grizzled approach to completing the task at hand, no matter the difficulty. That is not to say that there were not butterflies before each trip. Proper planning, weather monitoring, and equipment performance were critical pieces of a successful trip. Scott and Dave had learned through the years of mistakes that lack of proper equipment can lead to a much tougher hike. A proper pair of boots were essential, each had their favorite. Good socks as well. A lighter versatile pack with a solid reliable Camelbak bladder for water is absolutely necessary for a successful hike in the White Mountains.

With all that in mind, Scott took off from his Connecticut home around 6am. There was a little trepidation with his family as to hiking solo, but he assured them that he was confident and capable for such a task. In fact, he was looking forward to the challenge. The plan was to summit Mt. Jefferson, the 3rd highest peak in the Whites at 5,712 ft. No small order, but the weather conditions was terrific, a brisk, albeit breezy, sunny day. Perfect for climbing. The nexus of the Jewel Trail begins at the parking lot of the infamous Mt Washington Cog Railway, an iconic tourist landmark in New Hampshire. The Cog Railway allows tourists to climb the 6,288 ft Mt Washington aboard an historic steam and/or biodiesel locomotive. A truly memorable adventure for decades for families vacationing in beautiful New Hampshire.

Scott arrived in the parking lot before 10:00am, ready for the day's activities. As per custom Scott and Dave would often grill each other about pack inventory, ensuring nothing was forgotten. Careful examination of pack contents, keys secured, he set out to find the beginning of the Jewel Trail, having to walk through the visitor center of the Cog Railway. After utilizing the facilities one last time he set forth on this awe-inspiring trail; the Jewel trail is a popular choice for many iconic hikes in the White Mountains, including Mt. Clay, Mt Jefferson, and the ever-present Mt Washington. It was named after Sargent Winfield S. Jewell, who was employed by the Army Signal Corps on Mt Washington. It joins up with the incredible Gulfside Trail at 3.7 miles and 2,950 ft of elevation gain. It began with a steady, though not steep ascent through the hardwoods, distinguished by solid footing. After a mile or so it becomes steeper and a bit rougher and at approximately 4,000 feet the trail opens up, affording spectacular views of the Presidentials. It was an extremely cool, clear day, and surprisingly the trail was not that crowded with hikers. Scott had never hiked on this side of Washington prior and found himself stopping numerous times to take in the magnificent scenery. No matter which direction. Realizing that there was much work left to do, Scott

133

refocused on the task at hand. the trail was certainly becoming much steeper, rougher and he had to pay attention to his footing. Soon he met up with a father and son combo, resting along the trail, looking somewhat tired and a bit bewildered. The father and Scott began a conversation about each day's plan, and it was discovered that the two were headed up Mt Washington and possibly the Lake of the Clouds hut for the night. Scott inquired as to whether they had reservations, as the hut fills to capacity on most nights. The father replied that he did not. Short of telling the two of them to turn around, Scott gave them ample warning as to the difficulty of the remainder of the hike and the possibility that there could be "no room at the inn." However, it's always a welcome sight to see a father and son on the trails, tackling some the most difficult mountains in the entire Northeast.

Jefferson's Summit

After parting ways, Scott continued his rugged ascent up the headwall of Mt Clay, feeling strong and invigorated by the crisp mountain air. Soon he found himself at the junction of the Gulfside Trail, turned left and continued toward Jefferson. He had a little less than 2 miles to go, and soon realized that he was hiking on one of the most memorable and scenic trails in all the White Mountains. A flat trail, with beautiful views, it was if he was hiking on top of the world, no hyperbole intended. The weather was clear, cool and the scenery inspiring to say the least. It seemed that he arrived in no time to the summit of Jefferson, where he ate his sandwich, had an orange and gulped some water. The summit affords views in all directions, and the Presidentials never disappoint. Views of Monticello lawn, Jefferson Ravine and Jefferson Notch should be seen by anyone attempting hiking in the Whites. Having enjoyed the walk over from the Jewell Trail immensely, Scott did not spend a whole lot of time on the top and soon began his return. Soon he found himself back at the junction and began the steep descent back to his car. Scott completely lost track of time and soon met up once again with the father and son continuing on the Jewell Trail. Surprised for sure, Scott inquired as to their plans for the evening, and the father stated that the plans had not changed, the Lake of the Clouds hut. The day was getting long; Scott reiterated that that plan was ambitious (especially due to how slow they had ascended to this point). After carefully choosing his words, Scott instructed the father that he did not have to summit Mt Washington to access the hut, and it would be a bit easier and less time consuming.

The thoughts of the negative possibilities of the hikers dominated Scott's thoughts as he descended the trail and back to his car. Maybe he could have done more, maybe
not. Hoping for the most positive of outcomes, thoughts soon turned to improper navigation and the consequences of poor planning and possibly an unrealistic assessment of one's hiking abilities. All recipes for potential disaster.

Soon Scott found himself back at the Cog Railway and soon to his vehicle. After the ceremonial taking off of his boots, and a cold beer, he found himself wishing his long-time hiking partner was there with him to share the days' events. His thoughts soon turned to a strong sense of accomplishment. His first solo hike, avenging his previous disappointment of failing, and spending a magnificent day's hiking in the Presidentials was a feeling he would never forget.

It was time to shove off and soon he found himself sipping a tasty margarita and partaking in a delicious burrito at his favorite Mexican restaurant in Glen, NH.

There are many lessons learned from this days' events, notably that *even if you fail at something that is important to you, try again.* The sense of euphoria of accomplishment soon overrides any negative thoughts one may be holding on to. *Finish on a positive note.* In addition, accomplishing things alone is an enlightening experience, one that both Scott and Dave would relish forever. Many times, while hiking you really are alone, fighting to keep going, facing whatever negative thoughts that may invade your mind. *Mental stamina is one of the most critical factors in any successful hike and is most certainly a trait that can keep anyone ahead of the game of life.*

Next?

24. North and Middle Tripyramid

"The climb speaks to our character, but the view, I think, to our souls."
Lori Lansens

July 2009

The summer heat was on, and the hikers were getting itchy to get back to their favorite place on the planet. There was still a lot of work to be done and they weren't getting any younger so after a bit of pondering they looked at the Sandwich Range and decided the Tripyramids were calling. The 4th of July had passed, and they were both able to snag a little time off work so a two-night trip was planned, and they headed off towards the Hancock Campground on the Kancamagus to grab a site and enjoy an evening in the woods before climbing the next day.

There are multiple choices of trails to the Tripyramids of varying distances and intensities and the two decided to walk the Sabbaday Brook Trail for this trek. It was a little longer (4.9 miles one way) than the others and promised several stream crossings, but they chose this trail out of fondness of their memories of times spent at Sabbaday Falls many times over the years. They got an early start the next morning and when they arrived at the parking area there was only one other vehicle. Boots on, saddled up, and feeling good they hit the trail with hopes of standing on the summit of North Tripyramid within three hours. They were at Sabbaday Falls within minutes and took a bit to enjoy the beauty and roar of the falls where they had swum many times before. (Note: swimming is no longer allowed at Sabbaday Falls, sadly).

They had never really gone far beyond the falls in their previous visits and were looking forward to getting deeper into the wilderness as they came to the first crossing of Sabbaday Brook and quickly found that the water was quite high, likely due to some recent rains. Rock hopping here and staying dry looked to be near impossible but they knew from the Guidebook that the trail crossed the stream again just a little way up, so they opted to bushwhack along the bank to rejoin the trail upstream. However, in short order they came to yet another crossing and this time had no real option for further bushwhacking and very carefully were able to pick their way across without any falls or real wet feet. The trail from here was easy walking as it followed an old logging road for a while and made yet another easy crossing of the brook and began to ascend a bit more moderately. They came upon an old slide that appeared to be aptly named "The Fool Killer" and to Dave the name really seemed appropriate. From their point at the base of the slide it was nothing but a ridiculous jumble of rocks, boulders and gravel that appeared to go straight up. Being that it had nothing to do with the goals for the day, they both gladly passed it by and moved onward into the Sandwich Range Wilderness. However, just because they were able to pass up the Fool Killer did not mean that things weren't going to get rough for them about a half mile further up the trail.

Virtually every 4000 foot peak in the White Mountains finds some way to tweak a hikers nose. It can be any number of factors as Scott and Dave had discovered on their prior trips and climbs. It can be the weather not cooperating, or muddy stretches of trail, to boulder scrambling to the perils of improper preparation and they had experienced them all. This trail thus far had been a beautiful hike in the Sandwich Wilderness with moderate grades and overall good footing as it wended its way along the brook which some earlier visitor had adorned with Zen like cairns for over a mile long stretch giving it a bit of a mystical feel. Well, this all changed shortly beyond the slide at The Fool Killer as the trail steepened…. a lot! They still had about a mile or so to go to the junction of the Mt Tripyramid Trail and the trail turned meaner as the climb became much more strenuous as it ascended over a thousand feet in that distance over slabs, broken boulders, and roots. To Dave it was reminiscent of the Falling Waters Trail, that is, unrelenting up for as far as one could see up the trail. Scott had moved ahead a bit and as Dave came to any bend in the trail, he would peer around the corner so to speak hoping for some relief only to be presented with more of the same torture. It was not encouraging. However, onward they trudged and with no small measure of relief they soon enough found themselves at the junction with the Tripyramid Trail and took a well earned break.

It was decided that they would tackle North Tri first, as it offered no real views due to the growth of the forest at the summit. Being that this portion of the trail straddled the ridge between North and Middle Tri it was reasonably easy, and they made the half-mile to the 4180' summit in minutes and stayed only briefly before heading back south to grab Middle Tri and have some lunch. From the junction with the Sabbaday Brook trail it was only another three tenths, and they found their decision to do North Tri was wise as Middle peak offered much better views and (despite the cloudy skies) a nicer spot to relax and enjoy a peanut butter bagel and some trail mix.

Soon enough it was time to depart and work the way back to the car and a welcome night of camping, although both hikers were not looking forward to going back down that rocky trail towards Sabbaday Falls. They picked their way through it without incident and soon found themselves back on the more pleasant walk along the brook. Dave popped on his headphones and cranked up some Dave Matthews and said adios to Scott and commenced his somewhat customary downhill race back toward the falls and in less than two hours found himself sitting at the edge of the falls and soaking it all in.... almost literally as the water was high and the spray felt so refreshing. Scott arrived shortly after and off to the parking area for the customary congratulatory cold ones before driving the short distance to the campsite to enjoy a great meal and recap the trials of completing numbers 34 and 35 on their to do list.

The Tripyramids offered some nice views of the Sandwich Range and afforded Dave and Scott a reminiscent return an extremely scenic area on the Kancamagus Highway. It was place where we they been many times earlier, swimming, hanging out while camping at Jigger Johnson campground. Every trip at this time in their quest seem to involve 10 or so miles and that was fine with them. The mountains had prepared them for these longer trips, mostly in more remote areas of the White Mountains; these trips along the Kancamagus Highway offered both Dave and Scott some new experiences while returning them to one of their favorite sections in all the White Mountains. This was the first trip in which Scott's new purchase was introduced: an awesome Starcraft pop up camper. No more sleeping on the ground, no more tents, no more wet rainy nights in a sleeping bag. The remaining hiking trips became that much more comfortable as they also discovered the Hancock camping ground, set along the Kanc along the beautiful Pemigiwasset River. A hike in the mountains, followed by good food, a relaxing night by the fire could now end with a comfortable bunk, a well deserved good night's sleep, listening to the rushing river. Nothing more needs to be said. *"Roughing it" doesn't necessarily mean that one can't be comfortable.*

Full moon over the Pemi River

There weren't too many more to go, but the two were not looking that far ahead; instead, the focus was on what was going to be next. Still, lots more   work   to   do.

25. Mts. Liberty and Flume

"Colors are the smiles of nature"
Leigh Hunt

Fall 2009

It was the fall of 2009 and the two hikers had four peaks under their belt for the year; their thoughts turned to a return to Franconia Notch to tackle Mt. Liberty and Mt. Flume, completing the last centerpieces of one of the most memorable hikes in the entire Northeast. It was peak foliage, as well as brisk hiking conditions, all recipes for a great final hiking trip of the year as well as a comfortable night of camping on the Kancamagus Highway.

They arranged a couple of days off and headed north mid-week to avoid some of the leaf peepers and secured a nice spot at the Hancock Campground on the Kancamagus near the East Branch of the Pemigewasset River and set up camp under a starry sky on a cool evening, had a fire going in no time and settled in for an easy meal and an early turn in. By now the White Mountains were as close to a "second home" as could be and they were feeling comfortable and confident about the work ahead the next day.

Up at a reasonable hour Dave and Scott headed into Lincoln for a hearty breakfast at Flapjacks and arrived at the Liberty Spring Trailhead around 9:00am ready to go. Pre hike routines were like clockwork by now. The days' goal included summitting two Mountains, numbers 37 and 38, ascending out of the Notch via the Liberty Springs Trail. The day would include almost 9 miles, with over 3000 feet of elevation gain, as well as some good camaraderie and some awesome views. They knew what to expect as this was their third hiking experience to this area. As always, they consulted the White Mountain Guide to prepare further; they were expecting a steep and rough climb with poor footing at times.

Mentally and physically prepared, the two hikers set out on this crisp, clear day and initially set a pretty good pace as the trail remained moderate for a brief time. Passing the junction of the Flume Side Trail, the trail became a bit steeper without ever seeming to let up. Dave likened the trail to climbing a 3 mile stairway; these are the times while hiking when the monotony of putting each foot in front of another tends to wear on any hikers mind. You must pay extra close attention to each step; injury prevention is key. It was at this time that the two decided to "ease" the boredom a bit and play their usual game of geography. This particular game turned into one of their most competitive and lasting games to date; it still remains a lasting controversy as to who actually won.

Soon Dave and Scott found themselves past the Liberty Springs tent site and next to the junction of the Franconia Ridge Trail after 2.9 miles. Both were amazed at how quick and effortless the trek to the ridge was, citing the mental gymnastics of the game enabling them to free themselves from the drudgery of a difficult ascent. This stretch of the trail does not offer the same Ridge walking and spectacular views above the treeline as one gets heading north, but nonetheless it is a great walk in scrubby woods and a relatively easy wander to the summit of Mt. Liberty at 4459 feet. The reward for the days efforts was a spectacular view west of Cannon Mountain, the Kinsman Range and a northerly view of the Franconia

Ridge Trail. Looming south was their final goal of Mt Flume, and in short order both hikers were off working their way toward the final goal of the day. A fairly easy, uneventful walk across the ridge found them on the top of Flume looking at some of the most breathtaking views anywhere. The air was clear, the foliage colorful and the friends found themselves in a deafening silence immersed in all of Mother Nature's glory. *You learn to understand why the mountains are calling and why you go.*

Definition: Rooty

Soon, they could hear the chatter of a couple of hikers approaching the peak. As Dave and Scott looked over to greet them, they noticed that one of them had bent over and put a rock on a small cairn on the actual summit of Mt Flume. They were soon told that this was her 48th and final 4000 footer. Hearty congratulations were in order as they strengthened their resolve and determination to complete their goal and were extremely grateful to be able to share the experience with a total stranger. This was the second time that Dave and Scott were on the summit of a peak at the exact time another hiker was completing the 4000 footers. Coincidence?

144

Feeling refreshed, and filled with optimism, the two hikers began their return to Liberty and their eventual return to their vehicle. They cruised by Mt. Liberty and began their descent down the Liberty Springs Trail on a rapid pace for sure. Soon they caught up with the woman who had just completed her 48, and soon found out that she was with a hiking group, all women. They hike every week, different trails, different mountains; as they ascended the mountain with Dave and Scott the conversation was easy, thoughtful and each party learned a little bit about a person they had never met prior. A lot in common for sure. Similar to the hike up this trail, the climb down was extremely quick, both physically and mentally. In little time the entire group found themselves in the parking lot, saying their good-byes. It was an eventful trip.

Out with the chairs, off with the boots, they cracked a beer and began a long conversation about what they just experienced. Each trip was unique and each one meaningful in many different ways. The mountains were speaking to them, and who knows if they even knew it at the time.

A hearty meal by the fire, a chilly fall night under the stars, listening to the river, were the reward of the day. I'm not sure there was any need for conversation. Sometimes it's just better to listen. There appeared to be a trend with Dave and Scott's last few hikes. The physical challenges of each hike were no longer in the forefront of the minds; the discipline taught to them by each and every mountain had now transformed them to a place of total confidence (hopefully not complacency). When ones mind is no longer preoccupied with negative thoughts, it becomes more free and open to experiences only Mother Nature and what she is saying to you. They were in a good place as they contemplated the remaining peaks. Can't wait for what's next.

Flume and Liberty from Franconia Ridge

26. East Osceola

"I think nature's imagination is so much greater than mans, she's never going to let us relax."
Richard Feynman

May 2010

Memorial Day was upon them, and Dave and Scott were looking forward to another successful year; in 2009 they completed 6 peaks and their confidence and enthusiasm immeasurable as they planned back-to-back hikes, East Osceola and Tecumseh. Both mountains were located near Lincoln NH, relatively smaller in height and located in the Sandwich Range. Normally both Osceola and East Osceola are done together; Dave and Scott summitted Mt. Osceola in 2003 but ran out of time on that day and were not able to grab its brother to the East. There were fond memories of the view that day. Two "regulars" joined them for this 3 day getaway, Scott's brother Bob and old friend Russ. Russ also took his dog Hallie, a handsome German Shepherd who had been training for this hike as well. The plan was a two night stay at the picturesque Russell Pond campground on Tripoli Rd. The 2 trailheads were located practically across the road from one another just up the road from the campground.

  All systems were go, pre hike preparations, great weather conditions and the campers were packed with food, wood and plenty of refreshments for a great weekend in the White Mountains. An early morning start in Connecticut found the group at the campsite mid morning and in no time, camp was set up. With adrenaline flowing, the gear was checked, and the four hikers had boots on the trail by noontime as planned.

  The initial rocky footing of the Mt Osceola Trail did not deter the enthusiasm of the hikers as the banter flowed among life-long friends and soon they found themselves on a series of switchbacks leading to the ridgetop. As usual Scott had the lead, with Russ marching a bit behind and Dave and Bob easing their way up a bit further back. The 3.2 miles to the summit ledge passed easily and quickly they were all sitting atop the mountain enjoying some excellent views, some of the best in the Sandwich Range. After some congratulatory handshakes, and a nice lunch, it was time to finish the actual goal of the day, East Osceola lurking in the distance almost taunting them. Time for Dave and Scott to wrap up this "loose end ". Bob decided that he was satisfied with the one peak and began his descent alone. One thing to always keep in mind is the *wisdom to know when to call it a day*, to know when you've had enough, either physically or mentally. There were previous occasions when Dave and Scott turned back with the next goal in sight, including their next goal, East Osceola. No regrets, no feelings of failure.

Bob atop Osceola

Dave, Scott, and Russ (and Hallie) saddled up and headed down and east off the summit through a few rocky pitches and soon came upon a very steep gash in the mountainside called The Chimney; it presents itself as an almost vertical slide of rocks, gravel and unstable footing and it requires careful attention so as to prevent a fall or potential injury. Russ had to coach his 90 pound dog down most of the way and soon they found themselves on more stable ground and began ascending toward the summit. After climbing a few more steep sections the three found themselves on the wooded summit of East Osceola. Another one checked off the list, number 39. They were about to leave the summit when they were joined by another older couple who had ascended the peak from the Greeley Pond side, a trail off the Kancamagus Highway. It was number 20 for them. Congratulations were in order, hopefully they would all meet again on another mountain.

There are very limited views on this top, so the group made the quick decision to head back, after all, cold beer was waiting for them. In no time they found themselves back at the Chimney looking up at the daunting task of climbing back up toward their first peak of the day. With very little problem the three hikers quickly found themselves back on their first peak of the day, a much more crowded scene for sure. After some brief conversations with other hikers, and a final glimpse of the awesome views, the descent began. Dave popped on his iPod and headphones and said adios to his fellow hikers. To this date, the descent off Osceola was his fastest ever, culminating in just over an hour for the 3.2 miles trek. Scott and Russ meandered down the mountain at a slower pace, but still made good time. This trail gets very rocky toward the bottom and requires a bit more attention to detail. Soon however all four hikers met again in the parking lot at the trail head, a little sore, but all feeling extremely satisfied, and proud of the accomplishments of another great day in the White Mountains.

Deviating from normal protocol, the group made the decision to return to the campground for the post hike celebration. Substituting sitting by the beautiful Russell Pond and enjoying a frosty beer sounded a bit better than a crowded dirt parking lot. As always Russ suggested a dip in the icy water, an invigorating experience for sure.

Hiking mountains like the Osceola's was becoming fun for Scott and Dave. Not overly challenging, yet offering excellent views, are some of the many reasons this area is so popular with hikers of all levels. The mountains continued to call; hiking on Memorial Day weekend had become somewhat of a tradition for the two, many times joined by friends and family. A great hike on a beautiful day, ending with camping beside a pristine pond. *A great way to shake off the winter doldrums, get the body moving and get back to Mother Nature.*

The Chimney

After a hearty meal, and a warm fire, the conversation turned to the other half of the weekend goals; Mt Tecumseh awaited them tomorrow. Time for a good night's rest.

27. Mount Tecumseh

"Every mountain top is within reach if you just keep climbing."
Barry Findlay

Memorial Weekend 2010

The day dawned a bit later for the hikers, as they were all a little tired and sore from the Osceola trek, or perhaps they all had a few too many celebratory beers after a great day of hiking. Hard to resist for sure. Regardless, they wakened and were jump started by some Scott's high octane coffee, as well as a breakfast of sausage and eggs. Nothing like a little caffeine and some grease to get you moving in the morning. Packs ready, boots laced, the group was off for a short ride down Tripoli Rd to the trailhead of Mt Tecumseh, the goal for the day. The most popular approach to Tecumseh, the smallest of all the 4000 footers, is via the Waterville Valley ski area, but today they opted for the more convenient hike from Tripoli Rd, the Mt. Tecumseh trail. The ascent to the summit was only about 3 miles, with approximately 2200 feet of elevation gain.

The trail reports indicated that the trip would not be too strenuous, not a bad plan for consecutive days of climbing.

The hike began sometime around 10am, as they set out on a relatively flat logging road affording them the opportunity to get the leg, and muscles working again. Soon they found themselves at a small stream crossing and surprisingly despite the fact that it was early in the hiking season when streams and rivers tend to be much higher (snow melt), it was an easy rock hop across. As the group worked their way up the side of the mountain, they found the footing on this trail to be mostly boulder free, making for a more enjoyable climb for sure. The ascent became more moderate, and they found themselves navigating a couple of what the White Mountain Guide refers to as saddles; saddles, or what Dave and Scott call PUDS (pointless ups and downs) are described as the lowest area between two higher lands. Either way, these sections of any trail require descending which can be a bit of a challenge in the midst of any climb, resulting in more elevation gain and possibly another mental obstacle to overcome. If you're prepared for these, they most likely will cause only minimal issues. Pre hike preparation includes study of trail descriptions and current conditions, and always remains at the forefront of any hike in the White Mountains.

The hikers reached a much steeper rocky section of the trail as they were nearing the top when they were treated to a marvelous view of Mt. Moosilauke to the west. A needed reward for sure as they made one last push to the mostly wooded summit. A small cairn marked the top. Mt Tecumseh is a former ski area. Views from the top, which was mostly overgrown at this time, offered some fine views to the east, including the Waterville Valley ski area.

After a good snack and a brief rest, the four hikers started the hike down, looking forward to enjoying the rest of this beautiful day in New Hampshire. Off the steeper section, through the saddles, they found themselves in practically no time back at the trailhead happily completing 2 days of hiking.

It was only mid afternoon on this Memorial Day weekend and discussions ensued as to what to do with remainder of this beautiful day. Scott mentioned that he had read a bit about a group called Alpine Adventures, offering zip line tours. The crew eagerly agreed that this could be an interesting way to spend the afternoon.

They got there and found it not too busy on a Sunday afternoon and learned of the canopy tour, a series of five different zip lines in the hills a bit down I-93 and immediately jumped at the opportunity to join. A quick fitting of the harnesses as signing of the liability releases and soon they found themselves heading a couple of exits south to the rendezvous with the six-wheeler that would take them into the course deep in the woods. Once at the beginning of the runs they hadanother class as to how to hook onto the lines and what to expect as they landed. They were soon climbing the ladders and rope bridges higher and higher into the trees until they got to the launch point. There were a few moments of trepidation as Bob crossed the swinging bridges to the platform but once there it was certain there was no turning back. A couple of people went off before them, including one of the guides to show what to expect and next up Dave and Scott were hooking onto the lines and listening to the countdown to jump. As the guide counted down, "Three, Two," Dave jumped the gun on Scott and took off howling like a banshee. Scott was about a second behind him and amazingly silent but as the two descended he was gradually catching up to Dave because his larger size gave him more inertia and despite Dave's attempts to go faster Scott eased on past, while flipping him the bird as he went by. Bob and Rusty came next and as they came to the landing area the fire in their eyes and excitement was purely evident and almost childlike as they all raced to the next leg of the course. Four more runs ensued over different terrain, heights, and distances culminating in a last free fall drop BACKWARDS off a high platform to pump up the excitement just another notch. The entire experience was great and filled the afternoon and weekend with the right touch after a great couple of days in the mountains.

The group headed back to Russell Pond for a final night of good food, cold beer, and a warm fire. The weekend signaled numbers 39 and 40 for

Dave and Scott. They were both thrilled to be sharing these experiences with close family and friends while looking forward to another great year of hiking. These hiking excursions had become more than just routine trips up north. They became mental health days, providing them with a clear and proven way to escape the stresses of every day life; a distraction of sorts that required precise planning along with strenuous physical exertion. The lessons learned from each mountain provided Dave and Scott with the tools necessary to not only make each trip successful, but allowed them the ability to concentrate on other important things as well. *Turn off the television, put away the newspaper. Enjoy Mother Nature, she never   disappoints.*

28. North and South Hancock

"Well, you know, Boo Boo, I'm smarter than the average bear!"
Yogi Bear

June 2010

Another one of the Founding Fathers was calling, but this time not from the Presidential Range. Instead, the man with the largest signature on the Declaration was beckoning the hikers to the Kancamagus and challenging them to climb the peaks named Hancock.

Late June found a few days off for each and Dave and Scott packed the truck, hooked up the pop-up camper and headed north with their first goal being (appropriately) the Hancock Campground on the Kanc just a few miles east of Lincoln. They secured a site not far from the East Branch of the Pemigewasset River and with all their gained experience made the site a comfortable "home" for the next couple of days.

The next morning dawned a little humid and hazy but there was no rain in the forecast and after a quick breakfast and some of Scotts coffee they headed to the infamous hairpin curve on the Kanc and the overlook parking area where they would start on the Hancock Notch Trail, which for the first mile plus would be a simple and easy walk in the woods to loosen the muscles and get warmed up for what was to come. This mostly flat section was pleasant in that there were almost no rocks, but that was offset by the surprising number of roots that made the going a little slower from the effort of not wanting to turn an ankle. Despite that small obstacle they made it to the junction of the Cedar Brook Trail in a little over a half-hour and turned left to head toward the Hancock Loop Trail.

Things started to get more interesting through this .7 mile stretch however, as there were what seemed to be an inordinate number of stream crossings to deal with. Similar to what the men had come across on the Sabbaday Brook Trail it almost appeared that the crew who cut this trail many years before was toying with hikers by making them cross the same stream upwards of five times in less than a mile rather than simply run along the edge of the stream. The good news is that at this time of the summer the water was running low, and the rock hopping was easy as they scratched their heads and cursed as each new crossing appeared. Yet, no curse goes unpunished and as they picked their way across a relatively wider section of the brook with Scott in the lead, he managed to find one fairly large rock that decided to shift under his weight and after a few incredibly acrobatic maneuvers trying to maintain his balance, gravity took over and he plunged into the drink! As he was going down in what to Dave looked like slow-motion Scott tried one last ditch effort to right himself by planting his trekking pole to no avail and instead his body weight came down full force on the pole and snapped it in two! This was when the real cursing began as Scott extricated himself from the chilly water and made his way to the other side, while Dave did the best he could to stifle any of the roars of laughter that were welling up inside him. Fortunately, the only thing Scott hurt was his pride and after a few moments to calm down, check his pack and stow the broken pole, the hike resumed.

(Note: A portion of the Cedar Brook Trail has been relocated to avoid a few of these brook crossings since our hikers were there in 2010)

157

Shortly after Scotts gymnastics they came to the Hancock Loop Trail, and yet a few more stream crossings as the trail began to climb a bit more moderately and after a bit over a mile found themselves at the beginning of the loop to go over the summits. For no particular reason they opted to do this loop clockwise and turned left toward North Hancock.

Hancock Loop

It was here that the work of ascending a 4000 footer began. Up to this point, with the exception of all the seemingly needless stream crossings it had really been a nice walk in the woods on a summer day. However, one undeniable fact of the White Mountains is that eventually, every hike, *every peak is going to poke you in the eye in one way or another.*

158

The climb up to the peak of North Hancock is only .7 mile, but it is unrelentingly steep and extremely rough the whole stretch. The trail essentially parallels an old slide and goes straight up the side of the mountain over very rocky and in some areas sandy terrain with loose rocks. About halfway up, Scott paused for a moment and mused out loud about what kind of sadist would decide that this was the best way up to the peak. Dave concurred as the two trudged upward to a slightly less steep area before they achieved the 4420-foot wooded summit and a welcomed rest and snack.

The two didn't linger too long atop North Hancock as there was still some work to be done and they quickly set out to traverse the ridge over to South Hancock. The distance was only about a mile and a half, but there were several ups and downs along the way making the going a little slower than they had hoped yet they found themselves ascending the last section of the connecting ridge to the 4319-foot summit in only about 30 minutes. Another few handfuls of trail mix were shared with a gray jay while they sat and enjoyed the hazy view from a clearing near the summit before deciding that it was time to move on.

Rejoining the trail for the descent it soon became obvious that the walk down the mountain was going to be nearly as rough as the walk up. There was no slide and loose rock to contend with, but the half-mile down to the junction with the loop trail was tricky and sometimes bordered on treacherous with all the rocks and even more roots forcing them to pick their steps wisely to avoid a fall. It didn't last too long fortunately and soon they rejoined the much more forgiving section of the loop and Scott decided it was time to crank up the pace. Typically, it was Dave who set the tempo when descending, often leaving his companions in the dust behind him but this day Scott was feeling energized from a two-bagger day and took off quickly. Dave struggled at first to keep up, but he soon was gaining on Scott as they approached the Cedar Brook junction and the 1.8 mile walk back to the parking area.

Well, Scott wasn't having any of this as he picked up the pace even faster and soon broke into a trot along the wide trail. Stream crossings weren't about to slow him down now and he simply plunged right through them, disregarding any concern of wet footwear at this time. With about a mile to go Dave was gaining once again, jogging along to close the gap and was making progress as they approached the Kanc. As they climbed the little rise to get to the road Scott was held up momentarily by some traffic which allowed Dave to pull even as the two literally sprinted across the road in a mad race to see who got to the truck first. For fairness' sake, let's just say it was a dead heat as the two shared high fives and cracked the cold brews that had been calling their names.

This day they chose not to hang out in the parking area as their campsite was only a few miles down the road and they wanted to shed the wet hiking shoes and be able to sit around a fire later in comfort. Back to the Hancock Campground they walked down to the river to enjoy the peace and this time Scott went into the river voluntarily for a chilly swim. Dave opted out, choosing only to soak his tired feet.

Tonight was going to be another pasta and meat sauce night with some music playing, the fire burning a warm feeling of accomplishment from the day's effort, and a comfortable nights' sleep in the pop-up camper with a nice breeze blowing through the screened windows.

Signs currently in place

However, the excitement of the day actually spilled over into near dawn as the men were sleeping on opposite ends of the camper. Dave was awakened in the moments just as the sky was beginning to show any kind of first light by a noise right in their campsite. He looked out the window of his bed and heard some scuffling around and was barely able to make out a dark shadowy figure no more that ten feet from him. It didn't take long to realize they had a bear, and he was looking for his breakfast! Dave watched him in complete silence for a few moments while the bear rooted through their cooler and polished off any leftover pasta, parmesan cheese, bread, chips, cookies, etc. The animal picked up a cooler full of water and wasn't happy when he spilled it all over himself which Dave could tell from the disgusted snort the bear let out. As he wandered through the site looking for more goodies, Dave silently crept over to Scotts side of the camper and shook him awake and before Scott could move Dave whispered to him "We got a bear!" By now the bear had jumped up into the bed of Scotts pick-up and was essentially eye to eye with Scott as the truck was parked less than five feet away from where he was sleeping. Thoughts of "What do we do if he tries to get in here?" were running through both of their heads as they stood in silence; the only sounds being the bear scuffling through the site and the sounds of the two mens' hearts beating.

It was slowly getting lighter, and they could see he was no small critter as he knocked over the cooler full of beer and amazingly bit into one and drank himself a Bud Light! Dave was thinking to himself that the bear could have one, but if he went back for another that there was going to be a fight. A line has to be drawn somewhere after all.......

It wasn't much longer that the beast decided he had had enough and very slowly wandered off into the gathering light to pillage another campsite most likely and after about fifteen minutes the two guys ventured out of the camper to assess the bears' work. He was a hungry boy for sure as there was virtually no food left, and Scott offered that he deserved the bear beer because he obviously had a busy night. It wasn't long before sounds of commotion were coming from other nearby sites as the fat old boy made his rounds and was eventually chased off to seek his goodies elsewhere. *Remember, the animals were here first, and we are just visitors in their home.*

Meanwhile, they cleaned up the camp, packed up and went into Lincoln for an adrenaline pumped breakfast and even more memories to share of the past couple of days. Importantly, it was another lesson learned, as, even though regulations didn't require it at that time, the two learned that food (and beer) must be stowed and locked in a vehicle every night when camping in these woods. Fortunately, the situation never deteriorated into anything other than a very exciting wake up call, but if there were food stored in the soft sided camper it could have been a very different outcome.

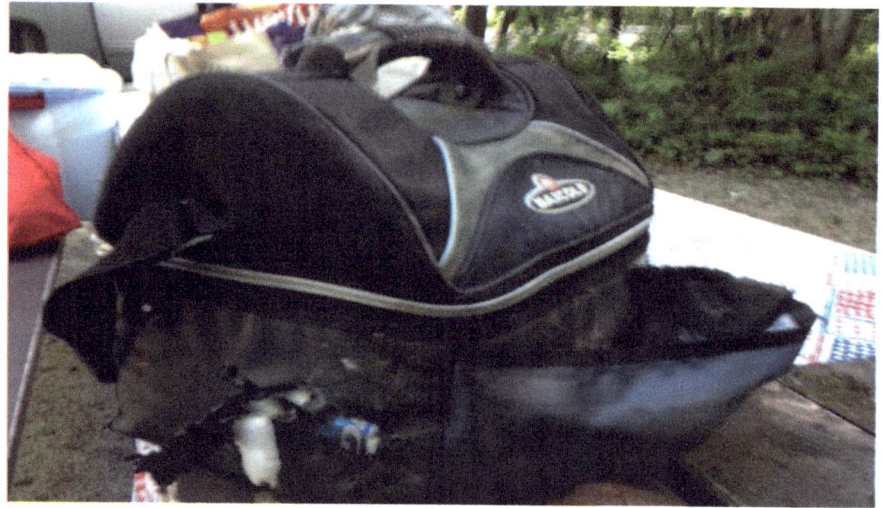

Ransacked cooler

Another couple of peaks in the books, and some memories to last a lifetime as they pondered the next trip for the upcoming fall.

29. Middle Carter

"You need mountains. Long stairways don't make good hikers."
Amit Kalantri

September 2010

The end of an arduous, yet thoroughly enjoyable quest to summit all 48–4000 foot peaks in the White Mountains of New Hampshire was nearing its conclusion. Dave and Scott had only 6 remaining mountains to climb to complete a pact they made almost 10 years before. They could sense what was happening but did not want to get too over confident. Every climb, every trail in the White Mountains has its own unique set of obstacles, and challenges. Dave and Scott respected this fact and continued to make precise preparations, considering local weather, trail conditions and their own mental and physical stamina. No short cuts.

October was rapidly approaching, and plans were made to travel to the Dolly Copp Campground for a weekend of camping in the cool autumn air, which would include a 10 mile trip up to Middle Carter

Mountain. This peak is a 4610-foot mountain, located along the scenic Carter Moriah Trail just north of Pinkham Notch. The Carter Moriah Trail is a 13.8 mile trail along the crest of the Carter Mountain Range and connects Gorham, NH to Carter Notch. It is home to four 4000 footers and includes many scenic vista's including the spectacular Mount Hight. Dave and Scott's original plan was to summit this peak 2 years earlier when they were completing South Carter; however, the weather on that particular day turned for the worse and they mutually agreed that the ominous cloud that was enveloping Middle Carter was enough of a deterrent to abort the trip. Dave and Scott were always in agreement that when it comes to potential bad weather, or deteriorating trail conditions, that they would always choose *"Safety over Peakbagging"*. Things can change for the worse at any time in the White Mountains; hikers must be aware and prepared for anything and everything that could happen on a hike and make decisions accordingly. One of their proudest accomplishments in their quest to bag all the peaks is that they were able to do them safely and without major injury.

The plan for the two was to embark early morning and ascend the crest of the Carter Moriah Trail via the southern terminus of the Imp Trail for approximately 3.2 miles, joining up with the North Carter Trail. From that junction they would ascend for 1.2 miles to the Carter Moriah Trail. From that point they would have a relatively easy .8 of a mile to the summit.

The days endeavor would include over 10 miles of hiking with close to 3000 ft of elevation gain.

The two left their favorite campsite at Dolly Copp around 7:30 AM. On this camping trip they were accompanied by Scott's wife Mary Ellen and his sister, Jackie They were not going to hike this particular time and planned on some other activities in the area. Plans were made however for a few beers, a nice meal together and a roaring campfire upon Scott and Dave's return.

With a bit of a fall nip in the air the two hikers began the day on the southern terminus of the Imp Trail, a rather uneventful 3.2 miles, crossing a few small brooks while moderately climbing toward the North Carter Trail. They were feeling well that day, and the trail offered some challenge, but overall, nothing notable. After the junction, at 3.2 miles and approximately 1.5 hours, it began to climb more steeply toward the Carter Moriah Trail. They knew that this would be the most challenging section of the hike, but on this particular day, the two breezed up the slope and soon found themselves on the scenic Carter Moriah Trail and an open area with beautiful views to the east. For the next .8 of a mile or so, they would find some open areas along the trail that afforded some beautiful views into Maine, Evans Notch, and to the west, the spectacular Presidential Range. Views were fleeting, but well worth the 2 plus hour effort. Soon they were on the top of Middle Carter, a wooded summit, offering little to no views. After a brief stay at the top, gathering in whatever remaining views to be had, the two began their descent. Looking forward to enjoying the rest of a beautiful autumn day and returning to the Campground were the remaining goals for the day. Knowing full well that this descent could be a bit boring, as well as the fact that they both felt strong, Dave and Scott began down on a bit of a mission. Many times, and on certain descents, one of them would say "Let's go" which meant increase the pace and hightail it back to the car. Dave would often lead the way, with Scott close behind, often trying to challenge Dave. Once the two reached the Imp Trail again, they knew the trail would be amenable to a 3.2 mile speed walk to the car. In no time they were done. The biggest challenge of this day nay not have been any part of the ascent, rather the boring 5 plus mile walk out. Mental stamina. At this time in the journey to bag all 48, Dave and Scott had taken in a wide variety of views, sights and sounds. Some beautiful trails, some not. All part of the journey for sure.

After the ceremonial removal of all footwear, a couple of ice-cold beers at the trailhead, the two made the short drive back to Dolly Copp. A few more well earned libations, a hearty meal and a roaring fire by a full moon were the ample rewards for another successful hike in the White Mountains. As their thoughts turned to the remaining few peaks, they were content with their decision to complete Middle carter on this beautiful day in October. The choice not to tempt fate and summit a few years earlier with ominous weather pending turned out to be a prudent and safer option. The mountains and the ever-changing weather patterns demand one's respect. Rather than look back with a sense of failure, instead the two focused on another extremely enjoyable day in the mountains, even if not one of the most memorable climbs. *The mountains may occasionally take from you, but they always give back so much more if you are patient and thoughtful.*

However, there is often a "little something extra" to add to the memories. Next morning as the small group was preparing to pack up, a small commotion arose near the meadow area of Dolly Copp Campground, very near where they were encamped. Mary Ellen went to investigate and came back quickly and nearly breathless. "There's a bear in the tree right across from us!!" That got the whole gang moving quickly as they went as close as they dared to get a glimpse. A young, but good-sized bear had climbed up into a crabapple tree and was having himself a fine, sweet, happy breakfast and he wasn't about to let anybody bother him. People all stayed back and let him enjoy before he descended and ambled back into the woods his belly full as he left the amazed campers behind. The whole campsite was buzzing with excitement, and Mary Ellen managed to grab a nice picture of the critter as he wandered off. This was Scott and Dave's second bear encounter, but certainly no less exciting. The four sat back at their campsite and as they nursed their coffees and chatted with fellow campers about the morning "wake-up call".

Mr. Crabby Appleton

As they began to slowly pack up, it was decided that their new bear friend needed a name. A few names were bounced around: Smokey, Yogi, etc. The usuals. Then Jackie popped out with "Crabby Appleton". The fact is that if a reader knows who Crabby Appleton was, then face it, you're old. However, as a more "senior" group, all present immediately knew who she was referring to and the name stuck. Another small lesson driven home: *One doesn't have to climb a peak to find joy, adventure and fun in the* *mountains.*

30. Mount Passaconaway

"We live in a fast-paced society. Walking slows us down."
Robert Sweetgall

October 2010

Late summer had slipped away, and autumn was in full glory in Connecticut and the urge to get back north for one more trek was gnawing at the men. Although the brightest of the foliage season had passed in the Whites, at least the leaf peepers would be gone while the hikers drove the Kanc to their next object of interest: 4043-foot Mount Passaconaway.

This would be a quick overnight trip without the camper in tow, as responsibilities at home didn't allow for a few days in the mountains, so an early departure from CT found them at the trailhead shortly after 9:00 to begin the 9.8 mile out and back using the Oliverian Brook Trail to the Passaconaway Cut-off and to the summit via Square Ledge. The weather forecast for the day didn't look great, as the skies were overcast and a little bit of early season snow was predicted, but nothing of any real concern. Temperature was in the low 30's and the guys made sure to have some colder weather items in their packs should they be needed. Dave had a knit hat and good gloves, a down vest and raingear as well as a supply of handwarmers should they be needed. Scott did pretty much the same as well as adding a couple of "space blankets" in case of any emergency.

Passaconaway is named for a chief of the Penacooks who ruled the area when the European settlers first arrived. Legend has it that the name means "Child of the Bear", which is a really cool name, but it made both hikers think of an earlier trip this summer and the bear encounters they experienced. By this time of the season both hoped that any local bears were curled up in their dens happy and sleeping.

The parking area was empty as they set off on the mostly flat and easy walk in the woods with good footing, although there were some fairly wet areas due to some recent rain, but that didn't dampen the spirit nor distract from what a nice section of trail this was to start the day as they covered the 1.9 miles to the Passaconaway Cut-off in less than an hour. There was even a little bit of "mood snow" starting to fall.

Bearing right on the Cut-off the trail continued as a nice easy walk with moderate grades and good footing for a bit longer before getting steeper as it crossed up the side of the valley. Despite the snow coming down a little heavier, there were a few glimpses of the peak through the mostly leafless trees.

The Passaconaway Cut-off offered what had come to be expected on every 4000 footer; that is, it started getting steep. What lay ahead was about 2200 feet of elevation gain over the next roughly three miles. The men had seen tougher climbs in the past, but this time the gathering snow offered a new twist and required some extra attention as they climbed. Their trekking poles were invaluable as they pushed on, helping to maintain the footing as the trail got a little rockier in the approach to the Square Ledge Trail. At the top of the Cut-off, the men had covered a distance of 3.6 miles in good time, but with the snow falling even harder they knew that the 1500 more feet of elevation to the summit would be a daunting task.

The next section of the hike would take them to the right on the Square Ledge Trail as things got rougher as they worked their way around a rock face of a cliff and picked their way over the rocks on the way to the junction with the Walden Trail for the scramble to the wooded summit.

One last push up the Walden Trail to a small clearing found our hikers on the wooded summit and to an underwhelming cairn marking another one in the books. Number 44 down and four more to go. There were options to take a few side paths to some various overlooks and views near the peak, however, with the snow falling and a tough descent for a few miles still ahead, the men opted not to stay and almost immediately turned around to head back to the truck.

By now there was about 4-5" of light fluffy snow on the ground, and they wanted to get moving should things start to become slick, or the trail become somewhat obscured, and they quickly found themselves back to the Cut-off and the walking got easier.

The beautiful part was the silence. There was no wind, they weren't close enough to the road for any sounds emanating from the Kanc, and it almost seemed that if one really listened closely enough, he could hear the snow hitting the ground. It was a lovely day in the hills as the two paused to soak in the scene and serenity. They slowed the pace to make the moments last and despite the temp dropping there was no real feeling of a chill setting in. Dave was wearing only a turtleneck Dri-fit and a sweater and Scott was actually sweating a bit, even with only a light jacket.

A few more miles and a couple of minor stream crossings over the snow covered rocks went easily on the Oliverian Brook Trail, and they soon found themselves back at the truck and thirsty and hungry. The choice today was to zip back to Lincoln for some burgers and beers at The Common Man by the fireplace and to "live it up" by not camping, choosing instead to stay at the Kancamagus Inn this night.

2010 had been another very successful year in terms of number of peaks submitted as well as the fun and adventures that had always drawn them to the White Mountains. These two weren't winter hikers in these mountains, so today was as close as they chose to get, and it was a satisfying and great day and just enough of a taste. They kept their snowshoeing and winter treks closer to home to keep in shape over the winter seasons as they pondered where they would begin the 2011 season.

Dave and Scott's quest to summit all 48 peaks over 4000 feet was nearing the end. Completing Passaconaway in the snow, late in the fall was a new experience that they relished. This mountain was not one of the more difficult treks, yet the snow added a new wrinkle and a touch of uneasiness. However, once again, confidence and stamina had replaced doubt and uncertainty with our hikers. This growth allowed them both the opportunity to savor the experience of hiking down a mountain under a fresh cover of snow, and to be alone with their thoughts. As they continued to learn, *there is not a more worthwhile exercise for the soul.*

31. Mount Cabot

"I wish I was a headlight on a northbound train"
Grateful Dead

May 2011

With only 4 peaks remaining left for Dave and Scott to conquer, plans were made early in the hiking season of 2011 to knock off Mt. Cabot. This mountain is the northernmost of all the NH 48, located near the Town of Berlin, NH. The plan of attack for this 4,170-foot mountain was to ascend via a short hike on the York Pond Trail, followed by 2.8 miles on the Bunnell Notch Trail, and ending with a rather steep 1.4 climb up the Kilkenny Ridge Trail to the summit.

Neither Scott nor Dave was familiar with the area, or the trails in the Pilot Range, but they were confident that the days strategy would be successful. On this endeavor, Scott and Dave would be accompanied by a large group of hikers including Scott's brother Bob, his nephew Luke, friend Russ and his son Derek and his friend Tony. After a delightful evening of refreshments by the fire at Dolly Copp Campground, the caravan headed northwest to Berlin early in the morning, arriving at the trailhead around 9:30 AM. The Trailhead is located nearby a fish hatchery, but there was no time for any exploration. There was work to be done. All preparations were made, packs filled with food and water, boots laced, as off the group went passing a small brook in an open overgrown, flat area. They soon arrived at the junction of the Bunnell Notch Trail; the trail was rather uneventful at the start, crossing a few brooks and remaining rather level with a few minor ups and downs. As the trail headed toward Bunnell Notch, it soon began to get a bit steeper, although remaining mostly moderate, as it climbed the remaining 2.8 miles toward Kilkenny Ridge. The group now turned right, up the Kilkenny Ridge Trail for the last 1.8 miles, and 1250 feet of elevation gain. This section of the hike certainly required more effort, but the group all appeared to be feeling strong and mentally and physically prepared for the day. Soon they would reach Bunnell Rock, a beautiful viewpoint of the Pilot Range south and west; as stated earlier, although Scott and Dave had hiked all over the White Mountains, neither had been here taking in these sights of Northern New Hampshire. After a brief snack, a couple of swigs from the camel back, the group now headed toward the summit and soon arrived at the Cabot Cabin approximately. 3 miles from the top.

The Cabot Cabin is located at an old fire tower, once serving as a fire wardens' cabin, and has provided refuge for hikers for many years. It is maintained by volunteers; sleeps about 8 hikers and is available on a first come first serve basis. A great place to spend a night, with beautiful views and a possible shelter from any inclement weather if necessary.

The last remaining .3 miles to the wooded summit was relatively easy and the group soon arrived on the top of the Pilot Mountain Range. Most of the nicer views were on the way up, especially near Bunnell Rock therefore there was little incentive to remain on the summit.

Hikers at Cabot Cabin

Feeling a sense of accomplishment, while knowing that there was work left to be done, the group descended for the remaining milage to the RV. It may seem obvious to any non-hiker, but a valuable lesson learned over the last 10 plus years of hiking, was the realization that when the summit has been reached, the days' work is only half over. The euphoria of stepping the top of these majestic mountains in New Hampshire many times will overshadow the work that remains on any descent. Climbing down can be anticlimactic, tedious and difficult on the already tired and weary legs. *Maintaining a positive, resolute mental outlook on the way down can be the difference between a positive or negative hiking experience.*

The trip down off Mt Cabot was uneventful; the only negative aspect of the descent was the wet, muddy trail which offered a bit of unsure footing. This was a minimal obstacle and soon the group found themselves back on the York Pond Trail feeling quite good about the days' accomplishment.

As they approached the last brook, Russ stated how he will be jumping in, as is his custom after each hike. Luke, the youngest member of the group began to cross the brook via an old log, when he lost his footing and clumsily fell in. After it was determined that he was not injured, the group had a long laugh on the young hiker which provided a humorous culmination to a great day in the mountains of New Hampshire. He provided us with a great memory for sure.

After a brief tour of the Berlin Fish Hatchery, the hikers arrived at their cars, took off their boots and had a few ice cold beers, and "debriefed" the days' activities. There is nothing like sitting in a comfortable chair, having a beer glowing in the sense of accomplishment with close friends and family. Scott and Dave had come a long way in the last 10 plus years, had seen and experienced much in their travels. But one thing for sure, is that moments like this never got old. Neither wanted it   to   end.

32. Mount Whiteface

" Well, I think we tried very hard not to be over-confident, because when you get overconfident that's when something comes up and bites you."

Neil Armstrong

June 2011

Scott and Dave were sensing the real possibility that they would be completing all 48 peaks in very short order in the summer or 2011. On that note they took off on a beautiful June day to summit Mt. Whiteface, located south in the Sandwich Range Wilderness. A quick trip, for a relatively small mountain, the days plan would be an early start from Connecticut with the goal of arriving at the trailhead on Ferncroft Rd in Gilford, New Hampshire around 9:00 AM for a 4.2 mile hike to the summit via the Blueberry Ledge Trail and Rollins trail. It would involve over 2900 feet of elevation gain, and according to the White Mountain Guide a few adventurous rock scrambles that would surely make the trek more interesting.

The day began as planned and after what seemed like a rather quick ride, the two arrived on time and began pre hike preparation. Food, water, and rain gear were the focus of their attention as weather reports indicated passing thunderstorms in the area. Not an unusual occurrence in the Whites.

One major item was missed however: each guy thought the other had packed the map of the area and yet somehow it was overlooked! By this time in their hiking and peakbagging venture, their confidence had grown, and being this was their 45th mountain attempted, they didn't expect any real wrinkles. This, however, would prove to be a big error.

It was a beautiful day in New Hampshire and the two started out along a gravel road to the Blueberry Ledge Trail bypassing the Dicey Mill Trail which leads to the Mount Passaconaway summit. The Bible of hiking in New Hampshire, the White Mountain Guide states "The trail crosses into the White Mountain National Forest and the Sandwich Range Wilderness, and at .9 miles continues straight where McCrillis Path to Whiteface Intervale Rd--not to be confused with McCrillis Trail to Mt. Whiteface". This short statement will prove later to be prophetic regarding the later day activities descending the mountain.

At 1.6 miles, the trail reaches the base of the Blueberry Ledges, and begins to climb moderately. It soon begins to rise steeply up the ridge, getting the heart pumping, and challenging both Scott and Dave, as was expected. This part of the climb did offer some excellent views of the Sandwich Range, however, the two encountered some very challenging rock scrambles, not entirely expected, which demanded total focus with a bit of anxiety for sure. After a couple of these scrambles, which involved removing their packs in order to throw them up the rocks, the two remarked how they were both relieved that the rocks were not wet. Slippery conditions on this part of the trail, would be certainly more dangerous.

Steep!

After negotiating the rugged climb and rock scrambles the guys soon arrived at the south summit ledges of Mt Whiteface after about 3.9 miles of walking. The views to the south were outstanding as they looked across the lower land towards Lakes Winnipesauke and Squam, but they quickly realized that nasty weather was impending, and their stay at the top would be a quick one. While they sat for a few moments, Dave took out his compass and got a rudimentary reading of their location and the direction back towards Ferncroft where they had parked. What prompted him to do that? It was relatively unusual the compass would come out, but on this occasion would prove extremely useful. They continued to the summit of Whiteface and shortly after returned to the South Ledges, contemplating their next move. Both remembered (maybe misremembred) that they had passed the McCrillis Trail earlier in the hike, and soon they were discussing a plan of attack for the descent. The memories of some rather difficult rock scrambles, and the thought of being caught on them in inclement weather, soon dominated their thought process. Without a map to refer to, discussions soon turned to a safer descent, possibly the McCrillis Trail. After all they had passed that trail earlier in the hike.

After a brief discussion they opted for what they felt would be a safer descent and began down the McCrillis Trail. The weather was going to turn worse, but both hikers were feeling strong as they began a rather rapid pace down the mountain. Soon they realized, possibly after a mile or so, that this did not feel right. Something was amiss. The two came upon a massive hoard of blown down trees. Climbing over and under the downed trees or trying to circumvent the blowdowns did no good. Each time they got beyond the trees the path was nowhere to be seen and no blazes were visible anywhere despite how many times they retraced their steps. Scott and Dave stopped for a brief moment to discuss their very uncomfortable situation and possibly change course; after a lengthy discussion with regards to climbing back up the summit and rejoining the proper trail, the two opted to continue downhill, hoping to find the McCrillis Trail again. The overwhelming belief that climbing back up the mountain would be exposing them to nasty weather while forcing the possibility of dangerous descents off steep rock scrambles was not appealing. They continued on.

Dave took out the compass again and said to Scott that if they bushwhacked a southerly course they were eventually bound to come back to Rt. 113, hopefully somewhere close to Ferncroft. They agreed this would be their best path off the mountain. Their confidence shaken, legs scratched from numerous downed trees, low water supplies and no map, the two continued their descent with an anxiety that they had not experienced to this point in the White Mountains. They continued through very muddy sections southward cutting across the ridges and going around a few large boggy areas. Both were in agreement that this was the best course of action, but thoughts began to enter each hiker psyche as to the possibility of spending overnight on the mountain if necessary. How much water and food do we have? We have space blankets, but will they suffice to keep us warm and protected? This could have been over dramatic, but when you're lost and worried all kinds of thoughts enter your mind.

With very little conversation, Scott followed Dave's lead; Dave had proven over the years to have a much better sense of direction. Despite this fact, the two continued to run into one roadblock after another, mostly in the form of "unhikable terrain." It seemed like hours had passed; beaten mentally they knew sunlight was waning but entertained no thoughts of quitting. They continued to alter their direction, navigating numerous obstacles while remaining on a southerly course. They were lost, bushwhacking through the Sandwich Wilderness when soon the two ran into metal fencing which indicated that they were closer to the bottom of the mountain. A welcome sight for sure. Relieved a bit, Scott and Dave followed the fencing, believing that it eventually run into someone's property. Feeling a bit of rejuvenation, the two regained their collective mojo, no longer feeling tired or anxious. Soon they would see a few houses, continuing along the fence line until they reached a road. Not sure where they were, the task at hand now turned to returning to the trailhead and the car. After a brief walk along a dirt road, near a few remote houses, a passerby stopped his vehicle and confronted the two weary hikers. He could recognize that they were lost, looking a bit weary. "Can you tell us where we are?" Dave asked. "Where are you headed" replied the driver. After Scott embarrassingly replied, "the trailhead at the base of Mt Whiteface on Ferncroft Rd.", the driver told them that they were not even close, and he would give them a ride. They were over 4 miles away from their destination. Embarrassed and relieved, they struck up a nice conversation with the gentleman and thanked him profusely for his efforts. He himself was a hiker and was sympathetic as to how things can turn for the worse while hiking in the White Mountains. Especially when you are not fully prepared.

Upon arriving back at the car, after taking off their boots and cracking a cold beer the two had a lot to discuss. How could this happen? Seriously. Never again would Scott and Dave be ill prepared for any hiking adventure, a lesson shared with many hikers they would share the trails with in the future.

Looking down at his scratched legs, sweat soaked shirt, and muddy boots, Scott broke out in laughter. Dave as well. What just happened? Relieved, and now more relaxed, the two now had a very compelling story to tell, And a very valuable lesson learned for sure. *Overconfidence and lack of thorough preparation on everyone's part can lead to trouble and potential disaster. Don't get too cocky. But don't ever give up.*

33. Owls Head Mountain

"The rivers flow not past, but through us, thrilling, tingling, vibrating every fiber and cell of the substance of our bodies, making them glide and sing."
John Muir

May 2012

The men were finally closing in on their goal of completing the 4000 Footers and vowed that 2012 was going to be the year to wrap up the last couple. For quite some time whenever discussion centered around which peak was next of their list, the "elephant in the room" always seemed to be Owls Head, a 4025-foot lonely hump smack in the middle of the Pemigewasset Wilderness. It wouldn't be ignored any longer.

Owls Head is a peak that hikers either love or loath. It is roughly an 18 mile round trip with several stream crossings and a rough scramble up yet another slide to get to the wooded, nearly viewless summit that on a good day can take upwards of ten hours or more to complete. However, the vast majority of the trip is really a lovely, mostly flat walk in the woods along several rivers and streams in beautiful solitude as far away from civilization as most hikers will get.

For this trip, Scott recruited his friend and co-worker Rodney to join in the fun, and Scotts' nephew Marc and his close friend Scott joined the crew. Being that this promised to be a long day, the group left Connecticut on a mid-week afternoon with the camper, tents, and enough food to feed an army with the Hancock Campground being the destination of choice. Arriving late afternoon, the camp was set up and the fire waiting to be lit as they enjoyed burgers and snacks and kept the beer consumption to a minimum. A 7:00 AM start was planned and after a quick breakfast and coffee they drove to the Lincoln Woods Visitor Center to begin the day. They paid their $3.00 parking fee, took an inventory (this time the map would NOT be forgotten!!) and set off into the woods by crossing the suspension bridge over the East Branch of the Pemigewasset River and immediately turned right heading upstream on the Lincoln Woods Trail.

For the casual hiker this is a beautiful stretch of trail that follows along the route of an old railroad logging bed leftover from the days of the John Henry Lumber Company that was last used in the 1940's. It is flat and wide and, in several areas, still has the old railroad ties that will cause an inattentive hiker to stub a toe. Having walked so many trails over the past ten plus years, our two hikers found it pleasant not to be ascending almost immediately, but Dave commented that it was almost borderline tedious…. straight and flat. However, that tedium was more than offset by the sound of the river and views through the trees of several nearby peaks.

After a quick 2.6 miles they came to another bridge, and crossing it turned left to join the Franconia Brook Trail to go deeper into the wilderness. Another nice, flat walk for a bit less than two miles, with some sections in boggy areas being crossed with plank walkways before hitting the junction with the Lincoln Brook Trail and turning left.

This is where things start to get a little interesting. In just a few moments, the group came to the first stream crossing of Franconia Brook. This crossing, one of two substantial river crossings can be quite tricky, and in times of high water downright dangerous. Being that it was late spring and had been fairly dry recently the water was, thankfully, reasonably low, but rock hopping would still be difficult. The younger members of the group, Marc and (young) Scott managed to pick their way carefully over the rocks and to the other side without getting their boots too wet, however the more senior members opted instead to remove their hiking shoes and instead don sneakers or sandals to wade carefully across using their poles. Knowing there was another crossing in less than half a mile they kept the wet shoes on for the crossing of the Lincoln Brook ahead. Another wade across, dry shoes put back on and the walk continued.

Deeper into the forest, the trail crosses Lincoln Brook three more times as it gets rougher and begins to present some various ups and downs as it first parallels the brook, then gradually rises above and moves away from the stream and approaches the junction of the Owls Head Path.

Up to this point, they had covered roughly 8 miles, and all were feeling good and strong as they took a break at the base of the path for a snack and hydration. They knew the next mile plus was not going to be easy. As he had said many times in the past, Dave warned the newcomers that every mountain has its own particular way of humbling a hiker.

The Owls Head Path is an "unofficial" and therefore unmaintained "herd" path that climbs up via a slide over very rocky and gravelly terrain as the path toward the summit. The path climbs quickly and steeply over loose rocks and hikers must be cautious not to dislodge larger rocks and present a danger to anyone below. About half-way up there are some open ledges that offer tremendous views of the Franconia Ridge peaks to the west as well as an opportunity to rest. The two younger hikers had forged ahead as expected, and Dave, Scott, and Rodney chose to take a breather and enjoy the sights on this clear day. As they moved on, Rodney was energized with being very close to notching his first 4000 footer and stepped up his pace with Scott not far behind. Dave, as usual brought up the rear, which was just fine with him. Another steep and straight pitch to a section where the trail moderated a bit and entered the woods again signaled that the peak was nearby. Dave was following the herd path alone and wondering if he had misplaced himself when he came across a sweaty cap hanging from a tree branch. He recognized it as Marcs and greatly appreciated the marker he left as he stuffed it in his pack and went to find the rest of the group. In another couple of tenths, he came to the small clearing with the cairn that marked the summit of this lonesome peak and rejoined the gang.

Marc had done several peaks prior, but for Rodney and Scott the Younger this was their first 4000 footer, and Scott was almost apologetic about there being no real view at the top. For the two newcomers it mattered little: they had walked nine miles through beautiful forest, fording streams and climbing landslides and the lack of a view was not going to dampen their spirits.

High fives were shared, and lunch was had as a few photos were taken and the chatter was animated about how great this was. But the afternoon was moving on and it became time to navigate down the slide and back into the forest.

There were sections of the slide that some members of the team opted to go down on their butt to avoid a fall or dislodging a rock, however it wasn't long before they found themselves at the base and the challenge was thrown down to see who would get back to the Visitor Center fastest. That was all that needed to be said as Marc and his friend took off, not to be seen again for a few hours. Dave popped on his headphones and turned up the tunes and disappeared as Scott and Rodney took a bit more of a leisurely pace.

Each person was experiencing and thoroughly reveling in the peace and solitude of this walk and despite some fatigue, feeling fully energized. The reason one feels drained after spending time in crowded places are the different types of energy required. Every person you pass, every advertisement in your face makes you focus differently and depletes your energy sooner. On the other hand, when one is in solitude or in Nature, the opposite happens. Your attention is drawn toward yourself and you

185

become filled with energy. When you spend time in Nature, watching the sun, the trees, the birds, hearing the wind and the streams, you won't get drained. Instead, you become rejuvenated because your attention is more centered and grounded. *Nature has no agenda, it simply is.*

The miles flew by on the flatter section of the trails, and the stream crossings somehow were not as daunting as they seemed earlier. Dave got to the point of fatigue that for the last few he didn't even bother to change his shoes, opting instead just to wade across and finish the day with wet, but not hot, feet. Once the turn was made back onto the Lincoln Woods Trail and across the bridge it was a sweet walk back along the river with a few stubbed toes on the railroad ties because of tired legs until all joined once again at the Visitor Center around 5:00 PM, where the younger guys were thoughtful and had already taken out the folding chairs and the cooler of beer for the arrival of the senior members of the team. It was greatly appreciated after 18 miles in ten hours as they collapsed into the chairs and shared their thoughts of the day.

Back to the campsite as a dinner of beer brats and kraut made by Dave's wife was quickly devoured while every cookie, cheese and cracker, and chip disappeared. If the ol' bear came along tonight he was going to be disappointed. Regardless, the coolers were stowed in the vehicles as the guys sleeping in tents didn't feel like bear rasslin' tonight.

Rodney was bitten by the bug and asked a thousand questions of this peak or that and he voiced that he may well decide to do them all. The two younger guys didn't go quite that far but knew in their hearts that if they were to attempt the feat, they would have no problems. The arrogance of youth....

The completion of Owls Head was a significant milestone for both Dave and Scott. It was their longest hike to date, and it was number 47. It was time to reflect on the events of the past 10 years or so, so many memories shared with so many family and friends. So many lessons learned. Owls Head had been discussed so many times, it was finally in the books highlighted by an 18 mile trip through some of the deepest, most remote woods in the White Mountains. The trip to Owls Head symbolized a decade of lessons learned, mistakes made and too many wonderful experiences to mention. Emotions ranging from absolute physical exhaustion to the euphoria of standing atop some of the most picturesque Mountains in the entire east. A sense of accomplishment with little regret or disappointment. So many quiet nights by the fire. So many pre hike preparations. It was time to reflect for both Dave and Scott. It had been an adventure they will remember for a lifetime. On to number 48, Mount Isolation.

Breakfast in Lincoln the next morning as Scott and Dave had put number 47 in the books. One more to go; Mount Isolation, and they wanted to turn it into something memorable.

After a hard day's work

34. Mount Washington & Mount Isolation

"Hack wide the belly of the swollen mountain and rip molten heroes forth from its furious spirit."
Van Morrison

July 2012

This was it: the end was in sight! After 12 years of taking and making whatever time could be found to get away to the mountains Scott and Dave were finally on the cusp of competing their goal of summitting all 48 peaks over 4000 feet in the White Mountains. A mid-July weekend was planned in hopes that the weather would cooperate, and the worst of the buggy season was passed, in addition to the fact that a sizeable number of people were invited to come along for the event and this timing offered folks a good chance to break away from work for a few days.

The Master Plan was to meet at the Dolly Copp Campground and grab a couple of adjacent sites for the campers and use it as the base of preparation as well as a great place to celebrate after what was hoped to be a successful journey. For this event there were a total of 12 people aboard:

some who had accompanied Scott and Dave on earlier trips like Bob, Rodney, Marc, Luke, Mike, and Scott the Younger. There were a couple of newcomers joining in: Scotts' wife Mary Ellen and Bobs wife Ann, Mikes girlfriend Amanda and Rodney's brother-in-law Don, along for his first 4000 footer. Like our hikers, all were in good shape and excited about the itinerary that was planned, which included an overnight at the Lake of the Clouds Hut.

The intention for this weekend would be to juxtapose the highest (and for many of the group, the first) peak they climbed, 6288-foot Mount Washington, with the (almost) shortest peak of the 4000 footers, Mount Isolation at 4005 feet. (There is some ongoing controversy about the actual height of the "shortest" 4000 footer, Mount Tecumseh, but that is an argument for another time.) Day one would consist of hiking up Washington via the Jewell Trail starting at the base of the Cog Railway to the Gulfside trail and Washington's summit before heading down for a night at the Lakes Hut. Day two would find the team cutting across the Camel Trail to the Davis Path to Isolation for the final peak and then down to Rocky Branch in the Dry River Wilderness for a 12-mile day to the lot on Rt. 16. A big weekend......

Both of our hikers had summitted Washington in the past; Scott on a couple of occasions with family members and a small group of friends in the late '70's and Dave twice, notably with a college class as part of the curriculum in Environmental Science when earning his degree. Both had hiked Tuckermans Ravine and Lions Head Trail so they were certainly aware of the effort that would be required. The Jewell Trail wouldn't be as steep as the trails on the eastern side of the mountain; however, it was somewhat longer. They both felt it was important to climb the "Rockpile" together to wrap up their quest.

Morning came early and the campers were stirring as the sky was getting light. Time enough for a good breakfast and a ton of coffee to really get the jitters going as the logistics were worked out regarding car spotting at the start and finish points. The plan was to be on the Jewell Trail by mid-morning, so the car spotters departed first, and the rest of the

189

group loaded up for the trip over to the other (western) side of Washington and Marshfield Station. All were accounted for by 10:00 AM, and they geared up and hit the trail as the Cog's whistle blew when departing up the slope of Washington. Hopefully a good omen. The sky was partly cloudy with the summit socked in, but the forecast for the day called for clearing and mild temps at the higher elevations.

The Jewell Trail enters the woods and begins ascending at a nice easy grade as the members of the team got the muscles moving and settled into their respective pace. The younger members moving ahead as expected with the newcomers not far behind and feeling the excitement while the more senior members set their own, slightly slower tempo. There wasn't a lot of scenery offered for the first three miles or so, but as they crossed through the scrub and hit the treeline the world opened up to see that there were some swirling clouds around Washington's summit as the trail became mostly large rocks and boulders as it steepened a bit more approaching the Gulfside Trail. Bob and Dave were walking together up this stretch with Mary Ellen not too far behind and as the two guys paused, Mary Ellen yelled up to Dave and asked how much longer is it like this? When she heard his response of, "Oh, pretty much the rest of the way", she let out a gasp and a moan of "Oh sweet Mother of God!" and as her shoulders dropped, she put her head down and soldiered on. As a matter of fact, this news seemed to galvanize her resolve and she picked up her pace and in short order passed Dave and Bob in what could best be described as "angry hiking". She flew the rest of the way up to the junction. Meanwhile, bringing up the rear of the contingent were Ann and Amanda, accompanied by Mike. The Marine in him wanted to tackle the mountain and show it what he was made of, but the gentleman in him and his spirit of camaraderie made him stay with the slower members of the group. This is not only a testament to the man that Mike had become, but *also a tenet of White Mountain hiking that no one is left behind, particularly when above the treeline.*

A right turn on the Gulfside Trail just south of Mount Clay led the hikers to the edge of the Great Gulf and though the peak was mostly in the clouds, the view into the Gulf was spectacular with the swirling mist sweeping up the slopes. Scott wondered to himself if everyone else was enjoying these sights as much as he.

Bob's legs were starting to cramp up as he and Dave made their way along this section of the Appalachian Trail toward the summit, so they stopped frequently for Bob to stretch and massage his legs while Dave encouraged more hydration. It was a painful and slow trek to the summit, but once Bob could see the goal, his pace quickened and soon they found themselves amongst the tourists who had either ridden the train or drove up to the summit of the highest peak in the northeastern US. The entire group rejoined in the restaurant after these two stragglers completed the 5 mile walk in a little less than four hours. A quick lunch was had and soon the group departed down the Crawford Path toward the Lake of the Clouds Hut arriving about mid afternoon to check in, reservations having been made weeks before.

They got one large bunkroom to themselves and changed clothing into more comfortable duds and shoes as a couple decided to take a quick siesta, others headed for the great room to relax, while others had even more ambitious plans. Rodney and Don decided that since they were so close, they were going to go bag Mount Monroe and Luke, Mike and Marc decided to join them and departed shortly after arrival at the hut. They completed the out and back quickly and were back well before 5:00 as dinner was being prepped by the "croo". A typical hearty feast was put out to the guests of the fully occupied hut, a bit of bourbon was shared as an after-dinner toast and the evening was spent in playing cards, socializing, and sharing adventures with other guests. Lights out was at 9:00 as the snoring and groaning due to tired muscles commenced.

Morning had the hikers awaked by the sound of a flute playing in the hall as the 'croo nudged the guests into consciousness and the smell of fresh coffee invited them to breakfast. Fully rested and fed, our group said farewell to the hut and embarked on Day 2; the day that our two companions would complete their quest. One exception, however, was that Bob's legs were very sore from the previous day's work and opted not to make the almost 12 mile walk planned for the day. He chose instead to descend back to Marshfield via the Ammonoosuc Ravine Trail, (no small feat in itself!) and guaranteed to meet everyone at the Rocky Branch Trailhead later today. He wished them well and took a solo walk off the mountain.

The sky was blue with puffy clouds as the group left the hut and joined the Camel Trail for a short traverse over to the Davis Path. The beautiful part of the morning was that the first 2 miles of today's walk would be above the treeline and the day was perfect for it. They basically had this section of trail to themselves, as the majority of hikers had other goals in mind such as summiting Washington or hitting the lower Presi's perhaps. They quickly joined the Davis path and skirted the edge of Tuckerman's Ravine towards the 5500-foot Boott Spur and gradually worked their way across a large open area where the trail could be traced off into the distance by the cairns laid out before them towards the scrub and back into the trees. Crossing over a nameless hump on the path, a junction presented itself that seemed a bit confusing. They knew that later today they would be utilizing the Isolation Trail, but this junction seemed "premature". A quick perusal of the map showed that this particular section of the Isolation Trail went off to the southwest towards the Dry River Cutoff and certainly was NOT the way they needed to go and instead they continued on the Davis Path. Based upon their Whiteface experience these guys knew to always make sure the map was carried and refer to it often to avoid any mishaps. In another .3 of a mile the portion of the Isolation Trail they would be walking later presented itself and confirmed the right choice made.

It was easy walking for another mile when a small spur path to the right presented with a sign placed high in a tree pointing up to Mount Isolation. It was here the gang regrouped and perhaps out of courtesy or respect the let Scott and Dave take the lead for the last few tenths to the summit. No amount of fatigue was going to stop those two from nearly running up the trail, with the rest of the group in hot pursuit. Scott the Younger was filming the two as they broke into the open on the rounded ledgy summit and Scott shouted out, "Is this it? This is it, Dave!!!" as the two embraced in triumph at finally achieving number 48. The rest of the gang arrived quickly, and hugs and high fives and handshakes were shared while pictures were taken of this moment of success with Mount Washington's summit in the clear sky behind them.

They lingered on top of Isolation for a while as our two Peakbaggers soaked in the moments and reflected on how long it took to finally get here. There was an almost bittersweet feeling in the fact that the job was done, and done (mostly) well, but when one of a person's achievements of a lifetime is completed, there is almost a small sense of loss once it's finished. However, that sad emotion was clearly outweighed by the elation of having joined a larger group of people who managed to forge their way to this point and that could never be taken away from them.

And there were still 7 plus miles between them and the Rocky Branch Trailhead and well-earned refreshments.

Back to the Davis Path for about a mile to the proper junction of the Isolation Trail which ran pretty flat and very wet, often right down a streambed by rock hopping for a few miles until they reached the Rocky Branch Shelter and turned right down the last stretch of the Rocky Branch Trail. It was here that the group spread out again, with Mike staying with Amanda and Ann, Scott and Marc walking with Mary Ellen and others taking off down the moderate slope. Rodney and Luke set the blistering pace and soon Dave and Don lost sight of them as the trail got steeper as they approached the trailhead. Soon enough one could hear road noise coming up from Rt. 16 as the last few switchbacks presented themselves.

Unbeknownst to anyone still up on the trail, Luke and Rodney reached the parking lot, threw their packs off and grabbed some camp chairs to relax while waiting for the rest of the group. As they were discussing the day Luke looked over towards a corner of the parking area and noticed a large figure standing on the edge of the brush. A closer look by both men made them realize this was something different for them.... a young moose was eyeballing them, and he apparently did not care for the two guys to be sitting in his lot! The moose began to approach them snorting and nodding his head in a threatening manner and quickly broke into a trot right at them as they ran behind a pickup truck to place something between them. Mr. Moose was having none of that as he chased them around the truck a few times while they yelled at him to try to scare him off. Rodney actually tried to take a couple of shaky pictures and perhaps the young bull decided he didn't want to be photographed and soon wandered off back into the brush as the two guys got their wits back about them.

Shortly after, the rest of the group began to arrive to find two wide eyed men babbling about a "moose attack" and being that this area was known for a sizeable moose population had no reason to doubt their story. With eyes on the edges of the lot the group set up their chairs in a circle and cracked a few celebratory beers and wondered if Bob would show up to join them. It didn't take long before he pulled into the lot and with a smile on his face presented the gang with two dozen Burger King cheeseburgers! Cheers went up and toasts were raised as the batch of fast food quickly disappeared amidst groans of delight. Bob knows how to please a crowd and he did it perfectly in this circumstance.

As the afternoon light began to wane it was time to retreat to the campground and settle in for a well-earned evening of rest. A couple of the younger members drove off to Gorham for half a dozen take out delights from Mr. Pizza and as the fire was lit the stories of the day were shared.

Scott and Dave were quiet. Over the past 12 plus years they had been coming to these mountains, summitting 48-4000 foot peaks, some more than once, and had walked several hundred miles in nearly all kinds of weather to complete their goal, and the magnitude of what they had completed was setting in. They were now well into their later 50's and this was likely to be the biggest physical challenge they would ever face, and although there were other goals that could be set, tonight was not the night to ponder the future. Instead, it was a time to enjoy the company of family and friends around them. The fire burned long into the night as soft music played and laughter emanated from the site with the warm feelings of success.

Mountain Whispers

Mike, Rodney, Scott and Dave, Amanda, Mark, Ann, Luke, Mary Ellen, Scott C, and Don

Atop Isolation with Washington in background

Others did join them while out on the trail,
And, as the years grew on many peaks they did scale.
With each new adventure, plans carefully laid,
Weather checked, directions made,
Through wind, rain and snow the mountains would show
If you took time to listen, soon you would know
That if you take heed, you will get all you need
Mother Nature is in charge, so stay on task.

195

Mountain Whispers

Her beauty is unfettered, no need to ask.

Scott Tetreault 2022

35. Lost and Found in the White Mountains

The Last Word

"Now he walks in quiet solitude the forest and the streams
Seeking grace in every step he takes
His sight has turned himself to try and understand
The serenity of a clear blue mountain lake"
John Denver

In 2012 we stood atop the beautiful Mt. Isolation with a group of close friends and family trying to make sense of all that we had accomplished. Number 48, at last. What a feeling. Staring across the majestic Boott Spur was the grandaddy of them all, Mt Washington majestically rising above the Presidential Range. It was the first, the highest and possibly the most difficult climb we had done, while standing atop Mt Isolation, one of the smallest. Although we knew we had an arduous descent ahead of us, the feeling of euphoria, and the sense of accomplishment was second to none. It was a great day for sure and we were elated to share it with those closest to us.

We've had some time over the past few years to think about our years hiking in the White Mountains. What we learned over time is that the mountains were speaking to us individually, yet collectively; both of us came to thesame conclusions about the lessons the mountains taught us over 10 plus years. That's why we wrote this book. The mountains don't yell at you; if you really listen, they whisper in your ear, but you must listen. Carefully.

We got lost in the mountains. Literally and figuratively. We took the wrong trail on numerous occasions, but never lost our way. Getting lost in the mountains had transformed into a whole new meaning. It meant we were in a place physically that we had never been before; mentally our focus became so intense that we became "lost" from the everyday stresses of life. No phone calls, no work issues, no traffic. Quiet solitude replaced noise and clamor. Getting "lost" on the trails was equivalent to a mental health day. Every so often life becomes hectic, and maybe a bit unforgiving, and a hike was a surefire way to provide oneself with the remedy. Climbing mountains became a way of adding balance to life, a cure all that unfortunately took us a couple of years to discover but was never forgotten.

Other things got lost in the mountains as well. The anxiety of a difficult climb, the apprehension of camping along beautiful mountainsides. Lost. Confidence replaced doubt, and soon we found ourselves capable, confident hikers willing to take on any challenges the mountains had to offer. Lost also were any preconceived notions about our inability to navigate throughout the many trails and trailheads throughout northern New Hampshire. Instead of becoming entrenched in a good novel, we spent hours upon hours "lost" in the White Mountain Guide, planning the next adventure, preparing for all scenarios as we planned our next trip. The mountains whispered to us that getting lost could be a good thing.

What did we find? We found out things about ourselves that we had no idea of prior to our adventures. Hiking can be done with others, but it is an individual battle. It's you against the trail, each steep section, each river crossing or each mud hole. Some days you feel strong, others not as much. You will fall, you will twist a knee or ankle, and you will wonder to yourself as to when each hike will end. You will beg to reach the summit only to realize that you are only half done. There is no one to get you through the difficult times except yourself. You find yourself and your physical stamina, you find your breaking point, and then press past it. Most importantly of all you find inner strength to complete not only each individual hike, but all 48.

What else do you find? You find many new acquaintances. You meet all kinds of hikers, and many of them provide some sort of inspiration. We have inspired others to hike the 48, and we've enjoyed hours on the trail with them. You find new equipment to ease your load and to make hiking more comfortable. You find that your mistakes make you stronger. And finally, you find a total sense of satisfaction in the completion of each hike; taking off one's boots, while relaxing in a comfortable chair and then reaching into a cooler full of cold beer after a hike is a feeling like no other. It never gets old. Blisters, a sore knee or ankle, and leg cramps aside cannot deter from the sense of accomplishment you feel, no matter how difficult the day.

As the song says, "regrets we've had a few, but too few to mention." One of our biggest regrets is that we didn't take enough pictures. We began this odyssey in the pre cell phone era, but that is no excuse. We took pictures but not entirely enough. We became obsessed with the arduous nature of the climb, weather and trail conditions, rather than the beauty that surrounded us. That isn't to say that we did not appreciate the views we were experiencing; the scenic views from the summits, the splendor of a rushing mountain stream and sheer magic of a mountain lake provided us with unforgettable moments for sure. Maybe we could have been more focused on Mother Nature, and not "making good time;" this would have been a better approach in hindsight. We had many climbs that we barely remembered the trail or the ascent, overly transfixed with speed and performance. Maybe that was our competitive nature, nurtured on the football field or basketball court. Another minor regret is wishing we had gotten an earlier in life start on this quest, and possibly affording us more adventures after completion. Age can certainly be a factor and needless to say that a Presidential traverse will not be in our future at this time.

Finally, we both wish we could have volunteered our time to assisting with trail maintenance. Maybe we still can.

However, these minor regrets pale in comparison to what we've seen, accomplished and experienced while hiking in the White Mountains. We have a renewed sense of proper stewardship of the White Mountain National Forest. We have acquired an ardent sense of gratitude to the caretakers of the trails, the thousands of volunteers who donate their time, effort and money to making the trails safe and accessible. We have become lifelong members of the Appalachian Mountain Club and have donated to various volunteer organizations like the Androscoggin Search and Rescue team. These conscientious individuals volunteer to assist in the search and rescue of injured or lost hikers. A noble cause.

The most important lessons we have learned over the years hiking, came from the mountains themselves and the whispers heard over time. Take time to breathe. Listen to total silence. Trust yourself. Open your heart to Mother Nature. Respect her. Don't take unnecessary chances. But most of all, listen. These are the lessons learned by a couple of middle-aged friends hiking in the vast wilderness of the magnificent White Mountains. *"We didn't realize we were making memories: we just knew we were having fun."* We hope you enjoyed the read.

36. Addendum

As even a casual reader may have surmised, the White Mountains of New Hampshire offer many challenges of varying degrees of difficulty, yet each trek and peak offer their own tribulations and rewards. There are so many factors that figure into a successful climb: things that can go as perfectly as expected, or things that can go wrong for no specific reason.

Therefore, the authors wanted to close by offering some insight into the groups that protect and preserve this magnificent area, as well as some basic insight as to how to prepare and keep safe during any walk in this incredible wilderness, particularly for someone who may be just beginning to explore the area.

There are two prominent organizations that administer the White Mountains, working under the auspices and in concert with the USDA Forest Service/White Mountain National Forest and the State of New Hampshire. The most foremost of which is the Appalachian Mountain Club. This group has been advocating for the preservation and maintenance of this area since the 1800's! Simply, the mission statement of the AMC is to "foster the protection, enjoyment, and understanding of the outdoors." They offer many educational programs, guided trips, as well as administer the hut system for hikers enjoying the high peaks.

The Hut System consists of eight mountain huts in the Whites, (several of which are above treeline), separated by roughly 6 to 8 miles of hiking for hikers who are looking to spend time enjoying the grandeur while providing sleeping accommodations and a dinner and breakfast to a weary climber.

The Randolph Mountain Club is similar to the AMC but focuses in the area of Randolph, NH. They maintain a network of over 100 miles of trails on the northern slopes of Mount Madison, Mount Adams, and Mount Jefferson in the northern Presidential Range. They maintain a system of four self-service shelters: Gray Knob, Crag Camp, The Log Cabin and the Perch. For the folks that prefer a little more solitude, these destinations are a great alternative to the AMC huts, but still while offering shelter and rudimentary facilities.

Any new or recent hiker must always remember the essentials to bring along on any hike in these mountains. We have seen too many people launching onto the trails who were woefully unprepared: mothers and children looking to climb Washington wearing tank tops and flip-flops, younger people ascending the King Ravine in tees shirts and carrying only a bottle of water with the intention of summiting Adams while very bad weather approached. The stories go on.

The facts are that any hiker (or group) needs to be prepared for what they face.

Any new hiker will find that it is best to start relatively easy and gradually work their way up to longer and more difficult hikes. Factor in overall distance (out and back!), elevation gain, conditions, and fitness level.

Find someone who shares your interests. Hiking solo is fine but hiking with a friend only enhances the experience as well as providing assistance should it be needed.

Learn to read a map and the basics of operating a compass. Fortunately, we knew that during our "misplacement" on Whiteface.

The State of New Hampshire Fish and Game Dept. offers a program called "hikeSafe" to assist hikers in gaining the knowledge necessary to venture safely into this rugged area. Through this offer, one can obtain a "Hike Safe" card indicating they fully understand the Hiker Responsibility Code:

"You are responsible for:
- Knowledge and gear. Become self-reliant by learning about the terrain, conditions, local weather, and your equipment BEFORE you start.
- To leave your plans with someone. The trails you plan on taking, projected start and finish times. You can write an itinerary and leave it on the dashboard of your vehicle as well.
- To stay together as a group. It's safer especially if you are not familiar with the terrain.
- To turn back if necessary. Know your limitations, weather changes, fatigue or injury can happen. It's ok to call it a day. The trails and mountains will still be there when you return.
- Plan for emergencies. Don't always assume you will be rescued; know how to rescue yourself.

Also, per NH Fish and Game: In New Hampshire, if you or anyone in your hiking group acts recklessly or fails to practice proper preparation as outlined by the Hiker Responsibility Code, resulting in Search and Rescue, you could be liable to pay the costs of your search and rescue mission. This is a law in New Hampshire.

Remember: follow "Leave No trace" principles. Stay on the trail whenever possible. Pack out all your trash…always. Pack a garbage bag and designate one hiker the "Trashman". There's no stigma in it. Sometimes, you just gotta go……. Do your business well off trail and bury it at least six inched deep. Try to avoid campfires. If you must, make sure they are completely DEAD OUT before leaving the campsite! Respect wildlife. "Nuf 'sed." Always let someone back home know what your plans are, what trail/peak your goal is, and what time you expect to return.

Simple rules, but crucial.

Essential items can vary ever so slightly depending on whether planning a day trip or an overnighter (or two) (or more!)

If a day trip, or an out and back to a peak, these items should be on your list:
1. A pack. If just a day trip there is no real reason to carry a full framed pack. A simple day pack will do.
2. Proper clothing. If the weather looks to be cool (check the summit forecast!) pack some additional warmer items like a fleece. If the weather is hot, some moisture wicking clothes. (Think a dri-fit or something similar.
3. Good quality shoes or hiking boots unless you want to end your day with blisters.
4. Plenty of food. High energy snacks, bananas, nuts, lunch.
5. More water than you think you will need. Yes, it adds weight, but after one episode of dehydration you will never forget it!
6. A map at minimum and the knowledge to read it.
7. First-aid kit. You never know.
8. A multi-tool and/or a knife.
(Optional): Trekking Poles. They can assist in climbing, and they can be invaluable descending, especially when the legs are already tired.

For a longer trip or an overnighter in the bush:
1. A larger pack if necessary.
2. Flashlight or headlamp.
3. Sun protection.
4. First-aid, and insect repellent. (You'll be happy you did!)
5. Something to light a fire if needed. (Matches, lighter, flint, etc)

6. Shelter. Even if not carrying a tent, at least something that can be used as a bivvy, or the knowledge and ability to build something.
7. Extra food.
8. Extra water. A bladder similar to a Camelback that nestles right into your pack is extremely convenient. (you'll be glad you did). Consider a water purifier like a Life Straw.
9. Toilet needs. It happens.
10. Rain gear. Never know.
11. A phone. Even though reception is often spotty in the mountains, it could be a lifesaver.

These lists may seem somewhat overwhelming, but over the course of our travels we found there were several times we thought we may have to resort to using some of them. One does not want to be deep in the Pemigewasset Wilderness or the Sandwich Range as darkness closes in and only them discover that it could be a long, cold, wet night in the mountains and to be lacking the basic needs. Better to be safe and at least somewhat comfortable, than miserable and sorry.

Please, enjoy your travels, but hike smart!

Dave and Scott

The 4000 Footers of The White Mountains

Mountain	Elevation (feet)
1. Washington	6288
2. Adams	5774
3. Jefferson	5712

4. Monroe

5384

5. Madison

5367

6. Lafayette

5260

7. Lincoln

5089

8. South Twin

4902

9. Carter Dome

4832

10. Moosilauke

4802

11. Eisenhower

4780

12. North Twin

4761

13. Carrigain

4700

14. Bond

4698

15. Middle Carter

4610

16. West Bond

4540

17. Garfield

4500

18. Liberty

4459

19. South Carter 4430

20. Wildcat 4422

21. Hancock 4420

22. South Kinsman 4358

23. Field 4340

24. Osceola 4340

25. Flume 4328

26. South Hancock 4319

27. Pierce 4310

28. North Kinsman 4293

29. Willey 4285

30. Bondcliff 4265

31. Zealand 4260

32. North Tripyramid 4180

33. Cabot 4170

34. East Osceola

4156
35. Middle Tripyramid
4140

36. Cannon
4100

37. Hale
4054

38. Jackson
4051

39. Tom
4050

40. Wildcat D
4050

41. Moriah
4049

42. Passaconaway
4043

43. Owls Head
4025

44. Galehead
4024

45. Whiteface
4020

46. Waumbek
4006

47. Isolation
4004

48. Tecumseh
4003

About the Authors

Dave retired from the Engineering Department of a major contractor for the US Dept of Defense in September of 2021. He currently has a nice job working for a local florist delivering happiness to people. He lives in northeastern Connecticut with his bride Tina. They have three daughters and a grandchild. Most of his hiking these days is done locally.

Scott retired from the State of Connecticut Department of Corrections after a long career as a Parole Officer. He is now working for the premier craft brewing company in New England pouring happiness for people. He resides in eastern Massachusetts with his wife Mary Ellen, and they have two children and four grandchildren. He is currently working his way through climbing the 52 With a View.

Made in the USA
Columbia, SC
13 February 2023

11853606R00124